BACK TO WORK

BACK TO WORK

A Guide for Women Returners

DIANA WOLFIN
& SUSAN FOREMAN

AvA4.

ROBSON BOOKS

First published in Great Britain in 2004 by Robson Books, The Chrysalis Building, Bramley Road, London, W10 6SP.

An imprint of Chrysalis Books Group plc

British Library Cataloguing in Publication Data
A catalogue record for this title is available from the British Library.

ISBN 1 86105 588 9

Typeset by SX Composing DTP, Rayleigh, Essex
Printed by Creative Print & Design (Wales), Ebbw Vale

While every effort has been made to ensure that the details in this book are up-to-date at the time of going to press, please be advised that the law, and employment practices and requirements, are constantly subject to change. Neither the authors nor the publisher can accept any legal responsibility for any consequences that may result from reliance on the information or advice offered in this book.

Contents

Acknowledgements

Many people have helped us in the preparation of this book. We would particularly like to thank Carolyn Brown of Finers Stephens Innocent, Sarah Graff at Taxing Nannies and Sharon Nash of Frenkels for their helpful appendices and especially for giving their time so generously.

We are also grateful to Rosemary Burrell, John Frenkel, Emma Golding, Corinne Gotch, Valerie Mills and Maureen Topping for their guidance and advice.

For allowing us to reprint material from their work, thanks are due to Steven Covey of Franklin Covey Co., Linda Emery of Unilever, Andrew Risner of Empowerment at Work and Francis Xavier University, Nova Scotia, Canada – Centre for Student Employment and Career Development.

Without the input of the many women returners and entrepreneurs who have participated on our courses, this book would not have been written. Students at the University of Westminster and Barnet College, as well as London Metropolitan University Guildhall have all made a significant contribution.

Finally, to our families we owe a great debt of gratitude for their constant encouragement and support.

Introduction

The idea for this book arose out of many years of running courses for women who had been at home with their families or looking after elderly relatives and wanted to take that all-important step of returning to the workplace. Countless women have sat in my office at the University of Westminster and shed tears over their lost hopes and aspirations which appeared to have gone down the plughole with so many bowls of washing-up water. How sad it is to feel that your task as a mother may be under control and that you want to return to work but you do not know how.

Not only do you not know how, you do not know if it is even possible. The world of work changes so very much in even a short time that it may seem like a foreign country to those who have been predominantly at their kitchen sinks for the last few years. Susan and I ran updating courses at the University of Westminster that offered the hope that there could be life after a career break. Women would say that just coming for the interview made them feel optimistic about their future: the chance to dress smartly, think about themselves and focus on their achievements was a rare luxury. They began to believe that they could re-enter the world of work, that they might actually have something to offer an employer. They realised that they were not alone in their frustration.

Before we start, I feel I ought to set the record straight about my own feelings on motherhood. I have four children whom I love dearly and who, along with their father and our two grandchildren, are the most important things in my life. I dedicated myself to them for all their formative years (and then some) and only after that decided that the time had come to return to work. I believe that nothing is more important than your children's upbringing and this book is not designed to bring dissatisfaction to the many thousands of women for whom child-rearing is totally fulfilling and rewarding. I found it so myself for many years.

This is intended to be a practical, self-help manual on what is required to make you more employable after a period at home when you feel that you are ready. I do not know when that time comes in your life – that is for you to decide. It will NOT guarantee you a job – I wish it would. That is up to you and how you apply yourself, and a small dollop of luck. The advice and information in these pages are practical and first-hand; they are borne out of dealing with many women on courses, speaking to countless others on the phone, undertaking research all over the country, and personal experience – I am a returner myself, as is my colleague Susan who has compiled the list of organisations which comprises the second part of this book.

WHO IS A 'WOMAN RETURNER'?

There is no such thing as a typical woman returner – your situation may be quite different to that of any other woman who has bought this book. The book has been written to help you if the task of bringing up your children leaves you wanting more out of your life, or if your children are old enough not to need the same intensive level of motherly involvement.

However, it is not only for women who want to get back to work after having children, but also for you if you have been at home looking after elderly relatives. This type of care also takes its toll on your confidence, as does being made redundant. Returners also include women who have come back from living abroad, either of their own choosing or having followed their husband's or partner's career. Perhaps you left work due to illness and are now fit and well, or maybe you have taken time out from the workplace as you are thinking about a new direction and want to see what is available to you. You may even have taken a 'gap year' to fulfil some personal ambition and are now ready to work again. There should be help for returners of all kinds within these pages. For women at home with children, though, there are the special issues of juggling your family responsibilities with working and coping with the emotional side of being away from your children; sorting childcare is a perennial problem.

The whole debate over whether women should combine their family life and work is not for me to cover – you have clearly decided that you are interested in working or you would not be reading this. We are rightly educating our daughters as we do our sons and must not be surprised that they want to satisfy their intellectual side by working. Or perhaps they are just financial reasons which make so many more women keen to return. We shall explore possible reasons why you want to go back to work in one of the early chapters but the wider debate is for another forum.

This book has chapters on the various elements that Susan and I think necessary for you to consider before attempting to go back to work. Not all of them will apply to you, but we hope that some will strike just the right note. The section at the back is for reference. It is as broad a list as we could muster of organisations, agencies, websites and anything else we could think of that we have been asked for over the years. We welcome suggestions for additions from our readers; details of how to contact us are at the front of the Directory section, see page 168.

We both hope that in your journey through this book you will find landmarks that will have a significant impact on your life and, of course, on the lives of those around you. It is our expectation that this impact will be a positive one and that, should you want to, at the end of reading it, you will make a smooth transition from being at home to being a working woman. We wish you every success.

Diana Wolfin

1

Getting started:
it all begins in your head

'A journey of a thousand miles begins with a single step.'
– Confucius

THE FIRST STEP

Making a life-change is a major step. Returning to work after a break
of even a year constitutes a life-change.

You may have picked up this book because you want information
on a specific aspect of returning to work (CV writing, interview skills)
or you may be thinking about the whole process and want some ideas,
as well as reassurance that you are not alone in how you feel after not
being at work. You may just want something for the bookshelf for
when the time is right for you to take that first step. As I write this book,
I do not have a picture in my mind of my typical reader – there is
probably no such thing. You might be a mother of three teenage
children, a carer for your elderly parents, someone who was made
redundant and wants to make a new start. Your age might be anything
from 30 to 60 and your education equally varied – you might have
come to the UK from another country to make a new life for yourself,
you might not have English as your first language, you might have had
a period of ill-health or have a disability and now be ready for a fresh
start. Perhaps you are married, with a long-term partner, either male
or female, with or without children – this book, I hope, will be relevant
for you all. You have much in common – all women, all thinking
about or even ready for a new stage in your life, probably all needing

a boost to your confidence in your ability to return to work, and possibly feeling that you are the only one in your situation. Having worked with so many women both in groups and on an individual basis, I have learned that there is no such person as a typical returner and yet you are all the same in some respects – I understand you as I was a returner myself. This is (briefly) my story:

Case Study: Diana
Having gained a degree in French and German, I gave up all hope of a career as a simultaneous interpreter when I married shortly after graduating. I worked for a while as a teacher and translator and gave up paid work completely when my children were born. When the youngest of my four children was eleven, I decided to enrol on a course at the University of Westminster, which was then offering FREE training for women returners.

On the first day, I was very anxious and felt a complete dinosaur as I did not even know how to switch on a computer. I was also very stressed as all four of my children had chicken pox in the week that I started studying and making arrangements for them was not something I had thought of. However, the course, which lasted three months, helped me regain the belief that I could offer something to an employer. After it was over, I started working on organising similar courses at Westminster, just two days a week at first, building up as the years went by and my domestic responsibilities reduced. What I could do twelve years ago is not the same as what I can do now, when my children are all more than twenty years old. And something meaningful can develop from a small start (i.e. two days a week). So there is hope!

OVERCOMING THE OBSTACLES

> *'One of the secrets of life is to make stepping stones out of stumbling blocks'* – Jack Penn

By looking at the negative side first, one can acknowledge the existence of obstacles and plan a strategy to deal with them. What are the problems – real or imagined – that a woman returner is likely to face when she says to herself, 'I want to go back to work'?

- Loss of confidence
- Loss of identity
- Loss of skills

These may come from her own feelings of not being able to 'hack it' in the world of work. These internal barriers need to be tackled before looking at external factors which may be beyond her control. Whatever the obstacles that apply to you, this book should help you to try to overcome them.

Loss of confidence

The most repeated phrase from women is, 'I've lost my confidence'. Whatever field a woman worked in before – whether at senior level, managing a large department with a great deal of responsibility, or in a less stressful job – she loses confidence when she has been out of the workplace for a while. It seems sad that confidence drains away so quickly when leaving work, but almost all women say this has happened to them. And indeed the same applies to men who have not been working for a while. So *you* are probably feeling the same way. You should take some comfort from the fact that your experience is endorsed by so many other women. Being at home with young children can sap your ability to relate to adults and this can contribute to feelings of isolation.

Regaining that confidence happens in a variety of ways, and the following chapters will provide strategies to help you renew the belief that you have something to offer the workplace. There are also case studies of real women for you to see what has been achieved. (The names have been changed to keep their confidentiality but the situations are real.) Confidence seems to accumulate like a pile of sand – when does it change from being a few grains into a significant heap? It returns in stages until suddenly you are in a completely different mindset, believing that you can succeed.

Case Study: Christine
Christine came on a women returners' course after a long period at home following the birth of her three children. She had previously

worked in industrial relations and was feeling a significant lack of confidence about going back.

Part of the course requirement was a two-week work placement, which the students tried to arrange themselves. Christine surprised both herself and us by reverting automatically to the use of her maiden name while phoning prospective placement hosts. In her mind, she was back in 'working woman' mode without being aware of the change. Her confidence was returning and the placement was a great success. She is now lecturing in her former field at a university.

Loss of identity

You may well have forgotten who 'You' are after many years of being viewed as your children's mother, or perhaps your husband's wife or your parents' daughter. Our sense of identity is closely linked to our self-esteem. This can be eroded if we see ourselves reflected through the existence of others and are not secure within our own self. Relating to ourselves through others is a common experience for women, especially when they have been at home for a while. How often have you phoned someone and said, 'This is Chloe's mother', instead of, 'This is Jane Smith'? Now it's time for you to regain your own identity and take time to develop yourself. This is the first part of getting your head around the change.

This may sound easy but it is, in fact, one of the most difficult parts of the process. For women who have been trained, perhaps even indoctrinated, to think of others first, it is difficult to focus on themselves. Guilt is ever-present and you will need to deal with this. If you have spent several years with your children, perhaps looking after your parents, or just putting your own needs on the back burner for whatever reason, you need to tell yourself, and accept it too, that this is the time for *you*. In the end, you will be happier and feel more fulfilled and those around you will benefit in many ways from your greater satisfaction.

Loss of skills

Lack of recent experience worries many women as they do feel out of touch when trying to return to work. What can I put on my CV? is a question often asked (CV writing comes in chapter 5). Offering yourself to a prospective employer for a placement period, unpaid, may give you much-needed current experience in a work environment and provide you with someone who can give you an up-to-date reference and recent work-experience for your CV. Although difficult to do on your own, it may be possible to obtain a short placement on a voluntary basis to get some work experience, rather like gap year students between school and university. It is surprising how quickly women can slot back into work mode as though they had never been away.

I also believe that working as a volunteer, either for a charity or some other organisation which has a need (meals on wheels, a Citizens' Advice Bureau, a charity shop, a local committee raising funds for a deserving organisation, becoming a local councillor or a magistrate – the possibilities are huge), gives you a chance to update or upgrade your skills and brings you into contact with other people from whom you can learn or look to as a role model. While I was not working I joined a local charity committee and over the years progressed from local and regional committees to national and inter-national level. I learned an enormous amount from my colleagues, many of whom were working women. To this day I appreciate all that I gained by giving my time as a volunteer. It was certainly more than I put in.

Feelings of low confidence are aggravated by loss of skills – these two are closely connected. Even following a fairly short break, the world has moved on a great deal, especially in the field of technology where knowledge is advancing at an alarming pace. Computer skills are essential in every field of work. Nowadays very young children can be so amazingly competent on a computer that you may be demoralised enough not to want to try. This very common scenario can be overcome with patience and the chance to learn computer skills in a non-threatening environment. Several organisations now offer basic computer-skills courses for adults with little or no knowledge. Some information can be found in the directory at the end of the book.

Jargon is ever-increasing and sometimes you might think that people are talking to you in a foreign language. Many of the new words are connected with the technology explosion or are management-speak imported into mainstream conversation – as we all know, language is a living thing, constantly changing and updating itself. Unfamiliarity with the 'buzz words' can certainly contribute to feelings of isolation and also to feeling out of touch. It is all going on 'out there' and you are not a part of it.

I can't do it

As I have said, some barriers to returning are in your head. Making a change does require a huge commitment and you will need to prepare for the mental shift in perspective that this may bring about. It can be easier to stay in a comfortable rut than to make the effort to move out of it. And it *is* an effort. So you need to get your head around the whole idea of it – the organisation required at home, the forward planning and the good time management necessary to sustain the role of the working woman, and the willingness to take a risk. It is not easy but there is the sense of achievement that goes with it (on a good day). We had better not talk about the bad days at this early stage!

EXTERNAL BARRIERS

> *'I have yet to hear a man ask for advice on how to combine marriage and a career'* – Gloria Steinem

The following rather negative points are, sadly, by no means exhaustive, but address the complaints made most frequently by women regarding the ease or otherwise of returning to work. Clearly we have less control and influence over such factors. This makes the task harder.

Ageism

We cannot ignore ageism as a barrier to returning to work. It is inevitable that a woman who has taken time out to bring up her children and is returning to work at over 40, will probably be viewed as 'older'. Some women have been told this as young as 35! Do not let it get you down; women significantly older than 50 have successfully returned to work, but if you give the impression of being out of date, irrespective of your age, you may be less likely to succeed. We inhabit a world where youth seems to be valued more than experience and wisdom, and we shall have to live with that as we cannot change it. Women with family responsibilities and the experience of managing those and themselves have a great deal to offer the workplace and the section on 'The untapped resource' (see page 59) will look at the particular benefits *you* can bring to an employer.

Looking your best

Appearance is very important in the battle against ageism and in boosting one's self-confidence. This does not mean trying to seem ten years younger than you are, but making the most of yourself and looking up-to-date.

- Check in women's magazines
- Observe women in the street who are obviously working
- What are they wearing?
- What does their hair look like? (a new style can make you feel completely rejuvenated and a new colour may make a world of difference)

These may be small matters but they can make a significant contribution to your confidence. Having interviewed many human resources (HR – formerly known as personnel) managers in the course of research at the University of Westminster, this point was significantly more important than we had anticipated. The way you look also defines how others relate to you and looking 'mumsy' is not appropriate in the workplace.

You may need some new clothes – this is a difficult area because money is likely to be tight, especially for single mothers and those who have been out of work for a long time. You may find it hard to justify spending money on yourself. However, viewed as an investment in your career, the outlay may take on a different perspective. In any event, if you are successful in getting an interview, you will need something appropriate to wear. You certainly do not want to be wearing what you wore five years ago, in hairstyle, shoes, clothes or make-up.

Make-up is a tricky issue. Some women do not wear it at all, but I believe that a little, well-applied and discreet make-up can give you a more groomed and hence more professional appearance.

Childcare

In general, the most significant barrier for mothers returning to work is childcare. In the UK there is still a long way to go in provision of the affordable, reliable childcare that enables women to return to work without worrying about their children while they are away, or being anxious about getting to work if there is a crisis at home. Research conducted at Westminster revealed (and you will not be surprised to hear this) that women with mothers who either live in or close by are those who make the transition back to working most smoothly. Sadly, not everyone can enjoy this advantage and many grandmothers are still young enough to be pursuing careers of their own and are not ready to stay at home looking after their grandchildren.

Your situation in terms of childcare may change after the birth of your second child. It is much easier to organise the care of one child than two or more and you will need to adapt your requirements accordingly. Women often think that it is younger children who need greater organising, but once your children are at school the after-school and other activities will need to be considered. It is also essential to keep an eye on your teenagers.

You can use a childminder if you are lucky enough to find one whom you and your children like. This is likely to be expensive, as are nursery fees, depending on where you live. Nannies or au pairs are other options but, as well as the cost factor, not everyone wants someone else living in their home or has the space for them. Many women find that their salary (after tax) is almost totally spent on childcare. This may need to be viewed as a temporary state of affairs and a compromise until the day that childcare is no longer needed. If a woman is working for a motive other than money (and there are many reasons, which we shall look at soon) then the expense can be rationalised more easily. If your motivation for returning is financial, and very often it is, then you need to do your sums to see whether it is indeed worth going back while your children are still young enough to need constant supervision.

Some employers – and not nearly enough – provide workplace crèches and they are a boon to the working mother. However, when that particular job is no longer yours, for whatever reason, the childcare ceases and some women prefer to keep these two aspects separate. The flexible working day is probably the best option but requires a far-sighted employer with a great deal of trust in you. The flexible working week also allows mothers a better option – it is easier to organise childcare for three days than five, for example.

Childcare options include:

- Nanny – live-in or share
- Mother's help
- Au pair
- Workplace crèche
- Nursery or other crèche
- Househusband
- Grandmother or other relative
- Friend
- Childminder

Location

Where you live may present difficulties if there is little demand for your skills in the locality or a general shortage of work in the area. You may need to consider travelling further (and take into account the extra time, cost and stamina required) or explore the possibility of re-training. Relocating is another option, although a drastic and rather expensive one. (A significant number of women have moved house due to their husband's or partner's work and find their own careers stalling on account of it. This 'trailing spouse' syndrome is surprisingly common.)

Choosing not to work

There may be pressure within your family for you to return to work and make a contribution to household expenses. You may really want to stay at home but feel that, not only for your family but also socially, you will have more status as a working woman. This is a difficult one, as the pressure to work can be very strong. Statistics (from the Women and Equality Unit) show that women comprise 44 per cent of the workforce and more and more are making the decision to return to work soon after their children are born. While this is fine for those who want to do it, the pressure on those who would rather stay at home is even greater. There is also the knock-on effect of so many other women working, in that there is no-one to see during the day as all one's contemporaries are away from home. The result can be increased isolation and loneliness for women who decide to stay at home. There are no friends to have tea with or to go with, accompanied by their children, to the park, which can only compound one's feelings of restlessness after a while. It seems to me that society does not properly value the role of the homemaker and educator of the next generation, which is sad. Women who want to be at home may feel that they have nothing to say at social gatherings (how often women declare 'I'm just a housewife'), and you may be influenced to work so that you can feel you are a worthwhile, contributing member of society. A generation ago this was not so often the case and women felt less discontented at home. Which brings us back to today's woman, deciding whether the pressure to return can or cannot be resisted.

Should you feel, after thinking it through thoroughly, that you are not ready yet to take that first step on your journey back to work, the time spent reflecting will not have been in vain. You will have learned a valuable lesson and the price of this book won't have been wasted. Knowing why you are at home and feeling sure that this is what you really want to do can give you the confidence to overcome the comments of others about your status.

Case Study: Stephanie

Stephanie had been caring for her severely disabled son for many years, until, very sadly, around the time of his twentieth birthday, Jonathan died. It was a very difficult time for her and her husband, as Jonathan had been their only child and the possibility of other children had long passed.

Stephanie's friends were all very supportive but many of them said to her, 'Now you can go back to work'. Originally she too thought that this was what she wanted and enrolled on one of my workshops designed to begin the return-to-work process. During that day, she had an opportunity to think seriously about what she wanted and not what other people were pressuring her into doing. At the end of the day, she had definitely decided that the time was not right for her to go back to work – she had not been waiting for her son to die so that she could resume her life. She decided to continue working for the charity which researched her son's illness and not return to paid work at the moment. Having taken the time to consider her own needs, she realised that there was pressure from other people for her to do something which she did not want to do. Spending the time at the workshop gave her the confidence to tell people that she was very happy with what she was doing and would consider returning to work when she was ready, which was not now.

After working with hundreds of women from all sectors of the workforce, I truly believe that more would choose to stay at home with their young children (say, under five years old) if they knew that there was a route back to work for them afterwards. The problem for women is that many of them, having worked hard to get where they are professionally, find that they have lost their place on the career ladder after being at home for a couple of years. More courses designed for returners at all levels would help women to regain their confidence and meet others in a similar situation, thus facilitating their success.

There can also be pressure in the reverse direction: a woman may be really keen to return to work and re-start her career but her family would like her to stay at home with the children. Such women feel that they will be better mothers if they are intellectually as well as emotionally fulfilled. They need to convince those putting pressure on them that everyone will benefit from the greater peace of mind they derive from being at work.

Either way, it is important to sit down and talk to those around you about how you feel. By sharing your feelings with them, they will be in a better position to understand why you are doing what you are. Sometimes it is a good idea to go out together to a restaurant or other public place as you will be more likely to keep your temper and deal rationally with the subject than if you were at home!

The way forward

Having looked at the barriers and realised that there are ways round many of them, you can now take a more positive view. Begin to consider the possibilities and advantages of returning to work, and see whether, for you, it is indeed worth the effort of doing so. The following chapters suggest strategies for coping with and resolving difficulties.

The good news is that employers are (slowly) becoming aware of the value that women returners can bring to the workplace, and are more willing to be open to different ways of working. The more enlightened approach of some employers to flexible work practices in general is having a beneficial knock-on effect for women like you in particular, especially for those juggling work and family responsibilities. Work-life balance has moved up the political agenda and many organisations are coming to appreciate that a more enlightened and flexible approach to the working day may not have a detrimental effect on their business. Quite the reverse!

2

Why do you want to return to work and where do you want to work?

'The difference between a successful person and others is not a lack of strength, not a lack of knowledge, but rather a lack of will.' – Vince Lombardi

WHY DO YOU WANT TO RETURN TO WORK?

It is very important to answer this question before you start looking for work in earnest as the reasons for returning will influence the kind of work you look for.

There are many reasons for returning to work and they are not all connected with the most obvious – which is 'for the money'. Of course, money is a factor in almost all our decisions to go into paid employment, otherwise we would continue with what we are doing, or devote our time to voluntary and charity work, which can be extremely rewarding.

Indeed, many women make the transition back to work much more easily if they have been working in the voluntary sector, as I have already mentioned; you acquire skills that can easily be transferred to other environments. The way an agenda is put together and the manner of conducting a meeting, whether for the school parents' association, or a local fund-raising group, or a business meeting at your place of work, are all essentially the same. I gained many skills from attending and later chairing meetings of a local charity group to which I belonged when the children were young and I was not in paid employment. When I returned to work, I already had those skills under my belt and was not lost at the first meeting I attended.

So, what is motivating you to think at this time in your life about returning to work? I have a list of about ten reasons and some or all of them may apply to you. There may be other reasons why now is your moment, but if you are able to take the time to assess your motivation for returning, it will help you when you are looking for work – if money is your main motive then you may have less choice in what you go for – the job is a means to an end. If you want career progression, for example, you may be willing to work for a smaller salary to gain the experience and for the prospect of something better in time to come. You may want to get out of the house, so take care not to choose something where they want you to work from home three days a week!

My top ten reasons for returning to work (in no particular order):

1) **Money** – the family needs another income to be able to survive and you are the one who is best able to get it. This is the most basic reason for working and is why many women return to the workplace.

2) But you may want to have **your own money** so that you have a level of **personal independence** rather than to provide for the family or contribute to the household's needs. This resonates with many women who feel that not earning money has disempowered them – they have to ask someone else for money for even the smallest thing, if they have a breadwinner around, or they have to do without. Both situations have a negative effect on one's confidence and as we live in a world where a person is often valued according to how much he or she earns, it is not surprising that a woman who earns no money feels undervalued.

3) You may want to return to work **to meet other people** and **escape from the isolation of being at home** without the company of other adults. However much you love your children, the conversation of three-year-olds may not be stimulating enough for you. Most young mothers now return to work when their children are still quite young

and if you are at home wanting to find other women to talk to, to socialise with, it is becoming increasingly difficult. In a previous generation, most women stayed at home when they had children and there were plenty of mother-and-toddler groups to go to, or other mums around to have tea or coffee with while your children were introduced to the skill of interacting with other children. Such mothers did not experience isolation and loneliness to the degree that I suspect women do today, so they are keen to return to work where they can meet others and feel valued.

4) This is also linked to **intellectual stimulation**, which is another good reason to want to return to work – being at home may just not be enough for you. This is a difficult area as many mothers and women who are looking after elderly relatives feel very guilty about wanting to go to work. This is especially so for the mother who returns to work and uses a childminder or crèche for her children. Somehow, if your child's grandmother is on hand, the guilt does not seem so strong. But with the dispersal of families and the continued working life of many grandmothers, this option is not open to many.

5) Perhaps while you have been out of work **you have gained another qualification** and may want to use it at work and **develop a new career**. It often happens that after a period at home, one's values change and returning to what you did before is not what you want. Many women feel that they would like to work in the not-for-profit sector and put something back into the community rather than work for a private-sector organisation where the 'bottom line' is uppermost in the company's mind. This often happens and entails targeting a totally new sector for networking and looking for jobs – and may mean a drop in salary from what was being earned before. This needs to be looked at while you are considering what to do – many not-for-profit organisations provide very high job satisfaction but relatively low pay. If you are clear in your own mind why you are returning to work, this will help you to decide if something is worth pursuing.

6) Returning to work may be a way of **regaining your self-esteem**. Many women have told me that their personal confidence has been at rock bottom after even a short time out of work (less than a year). They

feel like a non-person by being 'just a housewife' or a 'stay-at-home mum'. I feel that this is more a reflection of our society than of the ability of the women themselves.

7) Some mothers have also said to me that they wish to **set a good example to their children** by working. They seem to have less credibility at home because they do not work, and I am told that some children have even been known to say to their mothers, 'What do you know, you don't even have a job!'

8) **Timing** may be the reason you are looking to return. Perhaps something has happened to change your circumstances – you may be recently divorced or separated, or may no longer need to care for a relative you have been looking after. It could be that your children are now going to nursery, full-time school, secondary school or university; the days are long and you feel unstimulated and lonely.

9) Some women just want to **prove that they can** get a job and make a successful return to work, something that I often hear. It stems from a need for recognition and wanting to be one's own person and not just an extension of one's children/partner/parents. Women have said to me that they want to go back to work to show their children that they can, and that they are worth something because an employer is willing to pay them. So the pressure comes from within the home as well as from outside.

10) Women often feel that by being at home they have lost their sense of identity, of who they really are. They may be some-one's wife or partner, or Jack and Chloe's mum, but they want to be themselves, not reflected in the life of someone else. By returning to work in an environment where they are making their own way, on their own merits, they are able to **rediscover their sense of self and identity**.

Other reasons that women have shared with me include wanting to escape housework (with which I have some sympathy, although it seems to me that it is always there!), wanting to be needed, boosting confidence and needing a sense of worth (linked with self-esteem as well), to develop a talent, possibly newly discovered, to improve status and gain recognition, to face a new challenge and see that it can be achieved, or just for a different quality of life. Your reasons may be a combination of some of these, or just one, plain and simple. It does not matter why you want to return to work, but it is important that you identify for yourself why you are seeking a change in your life, as that will shape the work that you look for and everything connected with the job search.

Case Study: Fiona

Fiona had been at home with her children for about ten years. She had previously worked in the fashion industry where she had been a swimwear designer. When she was considering returning to work, she was looking for something that would get her out of the house and be a new challenge. She had been doing some small dressmaking and alterations jobs for friends in the interim and knew that she wanted something totally different. While on her career break, she had been called for jury service and found the court atmosphere very stimulating. She applied to be a court usher and was very pleasantly surprised to be offered the job. She had prepared herself by going to different local courts to get an idea of a typical day's work and by talking to a magistrate friend to get an understanding of the major elements involved in being a good court usher and the qualities the candidate would need. She applied to a relatively local Crown Court and was offered work that was flexible enough to fit in with her existing commitments and stimulating enough to satisfy her need for a challenge. The salary was less of an issue as she was not the main breadwinner in her family.

WHERE DO YOU WANT TO WORK?

The answer to this question covers more than one area. Where, geographically in relation to where you live? And where in terms of the type of organisation you might want to work for? Let's look at the geography part first.

There is no point in spending hours trying to work out what type of work you would like to do, only to find that there is nothing available within 30 miles of where you live. Unless relocation is on your agenda, and for some it may well be, you need to find work that fits in with where you live now. If you are organising childcare for the time you are at work, it also needs to take into account time spent travelling at each end of the day, both in terms of the availability of the child-carer, and the cost of the childcare.

Case Study: Natalie

Natalie began working in a nursery when her first child was six months old. The nursery had its own crèche facilities and the cost was reasonable. Although not earning a great deal of money, Natalie gained great satisfaction from what she was doing and did not feel that she was leaving her baby with a stranger, as she could see her at the crèche. She took maternity leave when her second baby was born and hoped to return to work.

However, when the time came, she found that the crèche fees had escalated greatly and her job had moved to the afternoons instead of the mornings she had been working before. This meant she needed childcare for her toddler as well, who was going to a morning nursery. She applied for other jobs that were in the mornings, but found, after calculating the cost of childcare from leaving home until returning, that it would be £5 a week less than the amount she would be earning. Taking everything into consideration, she decided not to return to work until her children were a little older and she would not need such intensive childcare. It was just not worth the hassle.

One strategy is to take a map with your home at the centre and, using a set of compasses, draw a circle with a radius of, say 10 miles, and decide that you will not work anywhere outside that area. The radius can be based on your preferred mode of travel, which will have a direct impact on how long it takes you to get to work.

Options for travel are:

Walking – the healthy option but probably limits you to about 2 or 3 miles' distance at the most, unless you are a champion walker. You need to take into account the vagaries of the weather and the state you might be in when you arrive. Are the clothes you would wear for walking suitable for your place of work? If not, are there changing/

shower facilities there? You could probably view the walking as your exercise for the day and that would free up the time you now spend on keeping fit (if you do!).

The advantage of walking is that you always know how long the journey will take you and are not subject to the stress of dependency on notoriously unreliable trains, buses, etc. The downside is that you have to have the energy for doing it. You have to be in relatively good health and you may have to carry papers or other essentials for work, as well as perhaps your lunch and other items. At the end of the day, when you are tired, you have to face the walk back, which might be somewhat unappetising in the winter when it is dark and cold.

If walking is not to your liking, what about **cycling**? Another form of excellent exercise, environmentally friendly and giving you the feeling of being in control of your travelling arrangements. It does require some courage, especially in inner cities where drivers have scant regard for cyclists, although some towns now have cycle paths alongside the road which can make riding a lot safer. You may arrive somewhat sweaty, so a change of clothes and possibly shower facilities would be useful. It can be thoroughly miserable when the rain is heavy or the wind blowing. However, for some it is a realistic option.

If **public transport** is what you would choose, think about the time you need to build in for delays and cancellations. If you are likely to work in an organisation where timekeeping is of the essence and there will be very little sympathy for lateness, you need to take this into account when considering the total time you will be away from home – not just the hours you are working. When I travel to the centre of London, I usually take a train which leaves half an hour earlier than the one I really need to get to my meeting on time – and often I am still late! This encroaches greatly on my personal time and I find it very stressful. Fares are also an issue – the cost of public transport will vary from place to place, but in south-east England local travel is very expensive. You may also be keen to commute – live further away and travel longer distances to get to work. The conditions of this travel – possible overcrowding on trains or buses, maybe having to stand all the way, arriving at work totally frazzled and exhausted – all these need to be added into the equation when choosing where to work.

If you are minded to **drive**, you need to be sure that the car you are using is not required elsewhere and that you are prepared for the stress of driving, the cost of petrol and the expense of parking. You may have a designated parking space and find that driving gives you 'time out' to think and be on your own – many people do. But the downside is long and stressful journeys breathing in other cars' exhaust fumes.

These are just options for you to think about when deciding how to get to work. You may not have the choice – and you may be thrilled to work anywhere and not mind about how you get there. This is fine too, and will help you to deal with any difficulties over travelling by rationalising that 'there was no other option'. My hope is that when you make the transition from stay-at-home woman to working woman it will be manageable and not add to your stress levels too much.

The next answer to the question, 'where do I want to work?' looks at types of organisation. Here are some thoughts for you to mull over:

Do you want to work in an office? A shop or other retail environment? With children or young people? Outdoors?
You may not have strong feelings on this, but it can be useful in trying to find out what exactly you want to do. Many women do not know where they could work or what kind of work they could do, mostly because they feel that they do not have anything to offer an employer and would just be grateful to get a job offer anywhere.

Try to think in what environment you flourish. Is your strength in organisation and could you be someone's right-hand person in an office environment? You may hate that idea and really want to work with people in a caring situation, perhaps a hospital or old people's home, or with disabled children. Maybe your skill is in selling and you see yourself in a shop working directly with customers. If you have a good speaking voice, telephone work of some sort might suit you. These examples are just to give you ideas if you are starting from scratch.

Do I work better with other people or on my own? Can I motivate myself without the support of other people?

If you have thought about self-employment, consider again your reasons for returning to work, as self-employment can be very lonely and you need to be extremely self-motivated and disciplined, especially if you start your business from home.

Do I want to work from home or is the purpose of returning to work to get me out and into the outside world?

If you have childcare problems, working from home to earn some money could be your best choice, provided that you will not be distracted by domestic responsibilities when you should be working. But you will save on childcare, so it may be a useful short-term option.

Would I like to work part of the time from home and part of the time in an organisation?

This is a good option: it brings you into contact with colleagues and can help with the feelings of isolation I have already mentioned, but gives you the flexibility to work from home should it be necessary. This may be easier to negotiate with an employer once you have proved yourself as the working-from-home part needs to be managed well. Your employer will want to be sure that you are doing the job properly and are not being paid to play with your baby!

Am I interested in working for a large organisation where there may be opportunities for training and development, or am I looking for a small organisation where I can just do my job and not take on too much responsibility?

If you are launching yourself into a new career, the prospect of training and development should be very attractive, providing the skills you will need to move it forward. Most organisations do have opportunities for career development (CPD = continuing professional development) and they sometimes state this in their publicity materials. Smaller organisations may not have the resources for T&D (training and development) and you may have to muck in, doing whatever is required of you. This could give you more practical experience and a chance to grow in an informal way. When you imagine yourself at work, think about what kind of place you see in your mind's eye.

What kind of business or area do I want to work in? Will it be an organisation where profit is the main objective or do I want to work in the not-for-profit area, or perhaps put something back into the community?

Consider whether you want to work in the private sector where the organisation will be very business-driven and profitability crucial. In a large law firm, for example, billable hours are vital to the firm's success. If you are more interested in the community and putting something back, you might like to look at the not-for-profit sector (charities and so on), or consider the public sector (local schools, hospitals, etc.).

Am I looking for permanent or temporary work? Would I welcome the opportunity to try out several different organisations to see what I am good at or what I really enjoy?

The first job you get after a period away from the workplace does not need to be a commitment for life. It will probably be a stepping stone to something else and a chance to gain some up-to-date experience and a recent reference. People move jobs much more frequently than in years gone by. Temping will give you a chance to experience working in lots of different organisations and may lead to a permanent offer.

Do I want a full-time job and all that goes with it, or is part-time more suitable for my present needs? Have I considered job-sharing and how do I go about finding out if an employer would consider this? Where do I find the other half of the job-share?

You may wish to consider a portfolio career, working part-time in several different ways, to make up a full-time job. This could be working for other people, or in a freelance capacity; for example, if you were a trainer you might conduct one-to-one sessions with individual clients or deliver training seminars in-house, with the possibility of writing on your subject for different publications.

Many women who come on my courses find that they provide opportunities, without dire consequences, to try out what it would be like if they were working. The courses I run for a local authority last twelve weeks, for three days a week. This leaves a short time to do all the things which the women were doing before and a chance to see whether other members of the family can deal with this new situation. At the end of the course many women tell me that they have found that they cannot work full-time until their family circumstances change significantly, and the course has been a brilliant way to test it out.

Are there any organisations that offer term-time only work which is stimulating and challenging?

Case Study: Rachel

Rachel had worked at partner level in a City law firm and was the mother of four young children. While her children were young she worked part-time and left because her husband, also a senior partner in a law firm, was seconded to his firm's Washington office. After several years they returned to the UK, and Rachel started thinking about returning to work as a lawyer. She thought it totally impossible that she would find stimulating work on her own terms: she did not want to work in the school holidays or at half-term, and she wanted a shorter working day to fit in with her children.

She had been an outstanding candidate before she had children but her confidence was at a low ebb when we talked about her returning. She felt that she was making great demands on a prospective law firm and did not have much to offer. We talked about the skills which she had gained both as a parent and when living abroad – her legal background was still strong; it would require a little updating but she could manage it.

Her CV did not do her justice and was rather apologetic about the time she had spent having her children and living abroad. She did some work on it to make those experiences more positive and she targeted several local firms with speculative letters, as she felt they would be more receptive to the dual role of mother and lawyer. She also applied for a job which was advertised in the Law Society's magazine, also for a local firm. Within a short time she had an interview, and a job offer with all her requests regarding her working hours met. As well as securing the job she had applied for, she was invited for interview by one of the firms to which she had sent a speculative letter. She had just not realised what she had to offer and had been focusing only on negative thoughts.

I have expanded a little on these rather basic questions just to get you thinking, but the answers for you will probably depend to some extent on why you are returning to work and your personal circumstances.

What do you most want from an employer?

Having asked all my groups this question, the word that occurs most frequently is 'flexibility'. When you say that you would like to work flexibly, what do you mean by this? The use of the word in the work context has been open to more than one interpretation. And it is very important that when you say to an employer that you would be able to work flexibly, you both mean the same thing.

For a woman returning to work, the concept of flexibility is linked to the unpredictability of her life and the hope that an employer will understand if her children are ill and she is late, or even does not come in that day. She might like to be able to go to sports day or other important events in her child's school calendar without it being a problem. In some ways this comes down to the organisational culture and how the work-life balance is perceived. (More about this in chapter 8 on work-life balance and coping strategies.)

For an employer, flexibility may involve understanding these aspects of a woman's life, but it may also include the flexibility to work late when deadlines approach; to take on other work when the situation demands it; to be prepared to 'muck in' when there are staff shortages or other crises. If everyone in an organisation wants Friday afternoon off or a long weekend by starting the week on Tuesdays, there will be serious problems in running the business. There can also be an issue when staff without young children or other pressing domestic commitments may not always want to work close to Christmas, in the summer when schoolchildren are on holiday or in other ways prop up the lifestyle of women with families. Flexibility should be available to all, regardless of the reason.

Case Study: Claudia

Following a six-year career break during which she had two daughters, Claudia returned to work full-time in the financial world, managing and monitoring projects and their budgets in the public sector. This was a position with considerable responsibility. Her daughters were still quite young at that time (three and five years old) and she really wanted to work flexibly. After a short while, Claudia negotiated a four-day week, to give her a better work–life balance. She had asked at the original interview what the organisation's policy was on work-life balance and knew that they might be receptive. They agreed to her request and she worked from Monday to Thursday, with a pro-rata salary. She too is flexible within this arrangement, and works on a Friday when it is imperative, swapping her days. She said it was just a question of 'having the confidence to ask' for flexibility.

Having asked many groups what they would like of employers, this is a selection of what I have been told:

- An organisational culture which accepts flexibility for all
- An interest in the job being done, not the hours present
- Training and other updating to help regain confidence
- An induction programme that takes into account a career break
- Rejection of the stereotype of 'mum' or woman returner
- Acceptance that women returners do have skills and the potential to learn more
- Recognition that women returners are eager to learn and are not afraid of development
- Childcare at work and an understanding of the position of the working mother/woman
- A sympathetic response to family crises and a willingness to allow time off to be made up to ensure the job is done

Some employers are already making a commitment to welcome women returners. Information on organisations which particularly recruit women or are favourable to women can be found in the directory at the end of the book.

SELF-EMPLOYMENT

This is a subject that could fill a whole book on its own. There is some suggested reading at the end of this book as well as information for the self-employed in the finance appendix, but there is a little I would like to say here about it, both from personal experience and from talking to others.

Many women are turning to self-employment when they think about returning to work. There has been huge growth in women's entrepreneurship in recent years; gone are the days when your local bank manager would patronise you, should you be bold enough to ask for money to start a business. But women are now also more pro-fessional in their approach to setting up and running their own businesses. They understand the importance of a business plan, have researched their market thoroughly and know how to balance their books. If you do not know these things but still want to be your own boss, there are many places you can go to get inexpensive, sometimes free, advice. My local chamber of commerce has a small-business service where accountants give their services on a regular basis and appointments are made where good, down-to-earth advice on setting up your own business is handed out.

This option is not for the faint-hearted. If you are doing it because you think that you will have more flexibility in your working life and not be answerable to anyone, it is important that you realise the reality of self-employment. Most people work far harder and longer in their own businesses than they do for other people.

You need to have a business idea – I belong to a group of women entrepreneurs and the range of businesses represented is huge:

handmade greetings cards
interior design
book publishing and retailing
beauty therapy
landscape design
motor trade
financial services
property investment
event management

public relations
translation
architecture
video services
employment agency
personal coaching
recruitment consultancy
bridal retail

The list is long and I have only given you a selection to get you thinking about options. Perhaps you already have an idea of what you might like to go into. But there is a world of difference between being an excellent beauty therapist and knowing how to run a business. You may need to be both. The network I belong to came together as a result of courses run by London Metropolitan University to help women move their businesses forward. So if you are thinking about running your own business, try to find out if there are any appropriate courses, ideally courses specifically for women. I cannot tell you how much I have learned from the other women on the course, as well as the hard business subjects which were covered (e.g. marketing your business, keeping accounts, researching the market). The network is also a great source of support and information for its members and has an online group which receives email requests and assistance.

In case you are thinking about starting a business from home – many women do until they are able to have premises – there are a few house rules you might like to consider:

- Decide what your working hours are going to be and stick to them
- Keep a dedicated space for your office and, if possible, a separate phone-line
- Some people dress as if they were going to work to make them feel as though they are at work, including wearing make-up and jewellery!
- Ensure that those at home know when you are in 'working mode' so that they respect your working time
- Train your friends not to expect you to have chats with them just because you are at home

- Do not get sidetracked by domestic chores when your business is quiet
- Be good at networking as you will need to do this without the daily contact with colleagues that working in an organisation offers you
- Make appointments out of the office so that you get out as much as possible – it can be a very lonely existence
- Get out every day for some fresh air – this will revitalise you, especially if your work involves a great deal of computer and phone work
- Be highly motivated, as all the work connected with your business will be generated by you. Being very organised is also important – make lists for each day/each week/each month
- Accept that there will be uncertainty connected with your business, which also includes financial uncertainty. It can take two to three years for a new business to be profitable and you need to manage the time and your money while you are growing it
- Having good health helps as you will not get paid sick leave or holidays, as you do when working for someone else. This is especially crucial in the early days when you may not be seeing much in the way of profit
- Be committed to long hours and hard work – you will probably work much harder for yourself than for a boss
- Understand what your responsibilities are to any staff you may employ, on however casual or irregular a basis
- Get yourself a good accountant and some sound financial knowledge. If you are not good at bookkeeping, pay someone else to do it, as it is an essential part of being self-employed
- If you are the type of person who likes to be in a 'buzzy' thriving environment, you may not be temperamentally suited to working for yourself, possibly on your own at the start
- Book time in your diary for your family and stick to it rigorously. It is easy to get carried away when there is an office at home. 'Just popping in for ten minutes' can stretch to a couple of hours and you may then all feel that your business is taking over your life
- Do not answer your business phone outside working hours. Have a user-friendly message on your voice-mail or answering machine (a personal message is preferable as the caller is sure

that they have got through to the right number – a new message every day including the date gives the caller confidence that you are in your office that day)

- Congratulate yourself if you have done well – there is no-one else to do so when you are working on your own and little treats can make a real difference to how you feel. Reward yourself with a break if you have worked especially hard and for a concentrated period

If you are using a computer in your business (and I would be very surprised if you did not), ensure that you have a proper back-up system and use it. When my computer contracted a nasty virus and all the files were wiped from my hard drive, I learned this lesson the hard way. I now have a CD-writer and regularly back up all the important stuff and keep it safe. Also check that your virus protection is up to date and do not open any attachments with emails unless you are sure that you are protected or know the source.

If self-employed, try to have a planned structure to your day or week as much as possible. A set routine will help you to optimise your working time and you will be clear in your mind when you are at work and when you are home, especially if they are the same place.

Owning your own business can be hugely exciting and sometimes rewarding, both personally and financially, but it certainly is not an easy option and if you are thinking about this for your return to work, plan it properly so that you maximise your chances of success.

3

The job search

'Be careful what you wish for, you might get it'
— ancient Chinese proverb

Finding a job is a full-time activity if you are serious about it. The truth is that a highly significant proportion of jobs are found by word of mouth (about 75 per cent, I am told) and you will need to be very inventive and focused, as time spent in your kitchen will not have put you in an arena where word of mouth is heard. You need to 'get out there', listen to what is being said and tell people that you are looking for a job.

It is also said that it is easier to get a job when you are in work. Many women take a job that may not be their first choice but which will give them a little up-to-date experience, opportunities to network, and be where word of mouth is heard.

You'll find a long list below of where information on jobs can be found – not all of them will, of course, apply to you, but they may trigger other ideas or give you strategies you had not considered. Hopefully, by the time you are ready to 'go public' with your desire to return to work, you will have a CV that you are happy to send out and a belief that you are able and willing to return to work.

The most common place to look for **advertised** jobs is in a newspaper. Here are the different types and what they have to offer. (A list of all the newspapers and which jobs they advertise on which days is provided at the end of this chapter.)

IN PRINT

National newspapers

These are issued daily, including weekends, and carry advertisements under specific headings (e.g. Secretarial, Management, Public Sector, etc.) on different days of the week. Because of the wide spread of their distribution, many of the jobs advertised will be geographically unsuitable for you. However, it is useful to see what the main requirements are for different types of jobs, and how many of these you can demonstrate. This can also be useful when you are looking at what to include in your CV, but do beware of just taking a list of criteria and reproducing them, as the reader will be able to tell that they have been lifted from an advertisement.

National newspapers will be suitable for you if you are looking at working in the City (London) or other major areas in the UK. You are less likely to find jobs advertised in your locality, but it is not impossible.

Local newspapers

Many of these are free, delivered to your home, usually weekly. Many local jobs are advertised in them, so if you are keen to work near home, they are very good places to start looking. There is also likely to be information and features on local businesses or people, which might stimulate you to write a speculative letter offering yourself for work. The free papers tend to have a significant amount of property and car adverts but they do have some jobs.

Paid-for weekly local papers sometimes have better journalism and articles, and more local job adverts. As a starting point, it is always worth looking at them and seeing what is going on in your area. If you do not want to buy the paper, your local library should have copies, as well as national newspapers.

Local magazines

Several free magazines regularly come through my front door, usually fortnightly. There is much to learn about what is going on locally from them: new businesses, information for women wanting to start their own businesses, local people looking for staff both in their homes and their businesses. They are an excellent source of information and, although they may not have a huge number of advertised jobs, it is worth looking when you are at the fact-finding stage of returning to work.

Free papers in central London

If you are living in the London area, there are a couple of free magazines and papers which advertise vacancies. Titles such as *Ms London* and *Nine to Five* are often handed out near Underground stations; *Metro*, a free daily newspaper, is also found on the Tube. You can also buy *The Big Issue*, a magazine produced to raise money for the homeless, which also carries job adverts.

Specialist magazines

Some professions are covered by a journal which will have job adverts connected with that profession; examples include *Nursing Times*, *Accountancy Age*, *The Training Journal*, *AutoTrader*, and *The Lady* (for nannies and carers). Trade journals, also clearly targeted at people already working in the field, often include vacancies and sometimes information on courses for returners to the trade or profession. The category also includes magazines produced by professional associations such as The Association of Women Solicitors, The Chartered Institute of Library and Information Professionals, The Pharmaceutical Society, and so on.

Some of these magazines may be available from your local newsagent, others come via subscription, or by payment of membership fees to an organisation. All will have useful information from time to time.

Voluntary organisations

Perhaps you have worked for a charity or other voluntary organisation while not in paid employment. Many of them produce magazines, both locally and nationally. They may be published less frequently, sometimes quarterly or monthly, but they may include adverts for jobs within an organisation that you know and to whose ideals you subscribe.

For example, magistrates have a monthly magazine; in between the articles and information there are sometimes vacancies. Hobbies you may have (embroidery, yoga, etc.) might well be covered by specialist magazines with a wealth of information, plus the added benefit that the subject is something in which you are already interested. Think about your interests and any publications connected with them – you may be surprised at what is out there.

Case Study: Jane

Jane had been working as a volunteer for the local branch of a charity raising money for victims of heart disease. She had decided that the time was right to return to work, but felt a great obligation to the charity and did not want to let them down. She realised that it would be unlikely that she could continue with her involvement and combine this with a new job.

When we talked about the kind of job Jane would like to do, it emerged that the voluntary role she was filling at the charity offered her everything that she wanted except money. I suggested that she talk to the people there and say that she wanted to return to paid work now; was there any possibility that the organisation would employ her? She would, sadly, have to reduce her involvement, or stop it completely, if she found a job elsewhere but she was very committed to the organisation and they would not need to train her at all! They offered her three days a week doing more or less what she had been doing before. Although money was not the most significant reason for returning to work, and the salary they were paying her was not very high, both the charity and Jane were thrilled with the new arrangement. Jane said that without talking it through she never would have had the confidence to ask about paid work within the voluntary organisation.

School newsletters

Many schools produce regular newsletters which the children bring home for their parents. In among the information about school outings and sports kit, staff changes and new regulations, you may find that the school is looking for staff – if I were in a school and this vehicle for communicating with parents was available, I would start with advertising vacancies there. Also, your own old school may have a magazine for 'friends of' or 'old girls'. They tend to have a long lead time for publication and to come out just once or twice a year, but there may just be a useful piece of information there, including what your old classmates are doing now!

Noticeboards and shop windows

Your local newsagent will have a noticeboard in the window. Among the cards advertising all kinds of services you may find something of interest to you, especially if you decide to work within walking distance of home. Perhaps you are good at sewing and a local dressmaker or curtain-maker is looking for help with an expanding business on a part-time basis. This might fit in with your plans if you do not want to return full-time to something office-based. There are also often noticeboards in:

- Your local gym
- The healthfood shop
- The local supermarket
- Your child's school, nursery or playgroup
- The local mother and baby group
- Your church or other place of worship
- Brownies or cubs
- Your local pharmacy/dentist/doctor
- The library, both local and specialist
- Local hospital
- Town hall

You could also advertise yourself via these boards (or in the news-letters listed above) but take care when doing so for all the obvious reasons, especially with the noticeboards in very public places.

AGENCIES

There are many agencies, both regular and specialist, to help with your job search.

Local Job Centres

I wish that I could tell you that this resource, set up to help people find jobs locally, was *the* place to go. Unfortunately, most of the women I know who have been there tell me that their experience was not the most positive. Mostly people go there who are receiving benefits and need to prove that they are available and looking for work. The Jobcentre Plus, as it is now known, is a government organisation for 'people of working age' (to quote from their website). It is also a service that will pay you the benefit you are entitled to if you are not working and will make sure that you are aware of all the benefits available to you and help you claim them. You can contact them by phone, via the Internet or face-to-face. They are not specifically geared to help women returning to work after a career break, but they will have jobs available which could be suitable for women returners.

Temping agencies

Returning to work by temping can be a very good way to regain your confidence, to have some up-to-date experience of the workplace, to secure a current reference, and to find out what you do and do not want to do, while earning money at the same time. It will suit those who are returning for the money and something to do and are not particularly worried about career progression. It is also a useful stepping-stone as it can showcase to an employer what you can do and may therefore lead to an offer of permanent work.

Recruitment agencies

There are agencies that specialise in particular sectors, for example:

- Office and secretarial
- Nursing and other hospital workers
- Accountants
- Nannies and other home helps
- Teaching
- Interim management
- Charity recruitment

They are paid by the client who is looking for staff, not by you – the person whom they place. Sometimes they receive a flat fee for the placement, or in the case of higher-level and permanent staff, a percentage of the annual salary. They take your CV (and sometimes help you with it so that it fits their 'formula') and present it to the potential employer, who may then ask to see you for an interview. If you require security clearance for work (e.g. working with young children or other vulnerable members of the population), it is a good idea to get that check done before you approach an agency (or an employer direct). This will save time and assure the prospective employer that you are serious.

Recruitment agencies vary greatly in their approach. Some are excellent; others raise your hopes and never find you work at all. It is hard to tell the ethical from the unhelpful, and for the novice in this area it might be worth asking around to see whether anyone you know has used a particular agency and with what level of success.

Headhunters

Headhunting agencies usually operate at executive level and target the right person for the organisation that is their client. Often, posts are not advertised but the person being headhunted is approached direct. While this is less likely to happen to someone who has not been working for a while, it nonetheless deserves a mention as a bona-fide way of finding work.

Citizens' Advice Bureaux

The CAB may have information about jobs available within the organisation in your area, and will be a very good resource to help you find out what is going on. They may also have details of voluntary positions, which might be a good starting point to gain some up-to-date experience and skills. Contact details can be found in your local library, town hall or via the Internet (see the directory at the end of this book for more details).

NETWORKING ORGANISATIONS

Many groups meet with the specific purpose of generating new business and making networking contacts. Some are breakfast clubs, meeting weekly to eat and promote their businesses (usually for the self-employed); some are women's groups which give support, both practical and moral, for women who are either working for others or running their own businesses. There may be such organisations in your area. Chambers of commerce have similar groups and your local Business Link may provide information on groups specifically for women. You can usually attend these meetings once or twice as a visitor without having to pay an annual subscription fee; for women who have been out of the workplace a while they can be a useful window into the world of work. You also gain information about local businesses which may be expanding or looking to take on more staff in other branches, etc. That kind of information could easily lead to work for the woman who is quick with a speculative letter.

RECRUITMENT FAIRS AND EXHIBITIONS

A day at a recruitment fair may prove to be time well spent in your quest to return to work. Keep your eyes and ears open to see when and where such events are taking place. National newspapers often sponsor these fairs, and will therefore give them prominent publicity. You can gain a great deal of useful information about employers and their requirements, on who is looking to recruit women, for example, and which organisations have family-friendly policies. Generally, admission is free and payment is required to attend their seminars. I have spoken at several of these on 'returning to work after a career break' and they are usually well attended.

The same tactics apply to **trade fairs** and any other events targeted at a specific area of work. Too numerous to list here, they are certainly worth attending even if they are not specifically geared towards employment or recruitment, as they will give you networking opportunities. It might be an idea to have some simple business cards printed so that you can hand one over if asked – so much more professional than scrabbling around in your handbag for a piece of paper and a pen (or writing on the back of a cigarette packet, which I have seen!). If you are not sure how to describe yourself, the card could simply have your name and contact details on it. It also might begin to make you see yourself in a different light, as you hand it over to someone. (Cards can be produced relatively inexpensively and there are some websites which will print them free.)

OTHER MEDIA

Jobs can be found on radio (both local and national) and television, and via teletext or cable television. Radio, while an excellent medium, is often listened to while you are doing something else; grabbing a piece of paper and a pen to jot down details requires you to be quick off the mark. Both teletext and cable TV advertise jobs; the large catchment area may mean that you are unlikely to find something in your locality – but it is not impossible.

THE INTERNET

More and more jobs are being advertised on the Internet, with email often being used both for CVs and application forms. This, of course, presumes that you are computer-literate and able to deal with applications in cyberspace. It also takes for granted that if you press 'send', your email will arrive. I would always send a 'hard' or paper copy and say so in my email.

Many websites are devoted to finding jobs online, and local authorities provide online information on jobs available in the borough. It is worth spending some time looking at what is out there, familiarising yourself with the terminology, expectations of online advertisers and what they are looking for from candidates. If they provide an application form, it may be worth printing one out to see how to fill it in. Such forms can be very restricting for the candidate who does not fit into the box exactly, and many women have felt daunted and not applied when they might well have been right for the job. See the chapter on application forms where there is guidance on how to fill in a form, both online and on paper. The directory at the end of this book lists some websites dedicated to providing information about jobs online.

Some government departments also advertise vacancies online and are well worth a look.

CAREERS GUIDANCE/ADVICE

Adult-education colleges, universities, local colleges and authorities may all provide career advice and guidance. Not all are geared specifically to women returners, but there are often excellent trained counsellors who understand the position of the woman who has been out of work for a while, and may be able to give information on updating courses or IT training, to give that extra boost to confidence. There are also private career consultants who give advice and do specific aptitude testing to help with the job search, but their services are usually expensive.

To find out about these departments, look for 'Adult and Continuing Education' departments at your local college or call your local education authority (details should be available at the town hall).

These departments may also run courses which can help to update your skills and increase your confidence. Having attended an excellent one for graduates who wished to return to work and then returned to work myself running courses at the same place, I am a big fan of this way back to work. Many of the courses are free to the participants as they are funded by the EU or the local authority. The participants gain so much from the course, as well as significantly increasing their personal networks by meeting classmates with whom they otherwise would not have contact. I am still running courses like this for a local authority and wish that they were available to all women who want to return to work. They offer an opportunity to test yourself in a non-threatening, friendly atmosphere, to 'fail in safety' as one of my students said. They can also be a real eye-opener for opportunities that you may not have thought of, and can also help you greatly to see yourself in a more positive light in relation to what you can offer an employer.

CONTACTING AN EMPLOYER DIRECT (OR COLD-CALLING)

There may be an employer you would really like to work for – what have you to lose by contacting him or her direct with a speculative letter and asking if there are any vacancies?

In such a case, preparation is vital. You need to do your homework, researching the organisation and its potential requirements, to ensure that your letter presents an irresistible opportunity to the employer. Never forget that recruitment is time-consuming and expensive – if an employer receives a letter from a suitable candidate and if the timing is right, there can be a happy outcome for both parties. In any event, you as a prospective employee have nothing to lose and everything to gain.

You may also want to approach an employer for whom you have worked before; this may be the easiest route back to work for those of you who want to do the same as before and where the organisation still exists, with people there who knew you when you worked there before. This is assuming that you left on good terms, of course!

To approach an organisation where you have not worked before, you will need to prepare yourself before writing the letter, and, most importantly, find out the name of the person to whom you should write. This is vital, as sending a general letter to a large department will not have nearly the same impact as writing to a targeted person.

How to research an organisation for both a speculative letter and preparation for interview:

- Start with people you know who work there, or have worked there. Find out about the ethos of the organisation, what is important to them as employers and think about what you can offer that they will find valuable
- The organisation may have an annual report, a website, recent press coverage (both good and bad)
- Your library may have information
- Television and radio
- The Internet, via a search engine, by keying in the organisation's name
- Newspapers, magazines and other publications
- Any in-house printed materials that the organisation may have

Try to find out:

- Is the organisation large or small?
- How many branches are there?
- Is it part of a group or a small, family-type concern?
- How many people work there?
- What is its annual turnover?
- Is it a growing industry or contracting?
- Is it an export business and if so, to which countries does it export? Do you have a connection with any of these that you could emphasise?
- Is it quoted on the stock market and if so, what are the shares doing at the moment?
- What is the company's policy on training and development?
- Does it have a diversity policy?
- Is it interested in recruiting women and has it in place any family-friendly policies?
- What is its record in terms of industrial relations?
- What kind of reputation does it have locally?
- Are there any political or other world events that could affect the business or organisation?
- Is it in the public or private sector?
- Does it aim to make money or provide a service to the public, or both?

Knowing something about the organisation to which you are writing a speculative letter will increase your confidence and provide you with the chance to show that you have done your homework and are taking the trouble to research its business. It will add to your credibility if you include in the letter a relevant piece of information that shows you have already begun to take a real interest in the organisation, rather than focusing on what *you* want.

The chapter on application forms also has some details on how to write a speculative letter.

YOUR OWN NETWORKING

As has already been mentioned, networking is the main way that people find jobs – they hear about someone leaving for a new job or going on maternity leave, and perhaps someone puts in a good word for them within the organisation. This is networking at its simplest level. In order for it to work for you, you need to be aware of where your networks are, and have some idea of what you would like to do, as you will need to respond to an offer of help with confidence.

Where are your networks if you have been out of work for some while?

- Your children's schools
- Your local community
- Your gym or sports club
- Your hairdresser
- Your family and friends
- Friends of your family and friends
- Social clubs you belong to
- People you know through your hobbies
- Voluntary organisations for which you work

Case Study: Helen
Helen was on a course where part of the requirement was a four-week work-placement to gain up-to-date experience while working on a project of some value to the host. Previously a teacher, Helen did not want to return to teaching but to do something connected with

schools and teaching. Following extensive research, she decided that she would like to work at the Education Department of the British Museum. I had no contact there, but Helen revealed, when pressed, that the head of the department had a child at her child's school. I suggested that she talk to him at the school gate and ask for a placement. She had not thought of this and felt that she was taking advantage of her connection which would be frowned upon.

It was agreed that she would approach her contact by saying that she was doing a course and a placement was part of it. As she would love to spend four weeks in the Education Department, could she ring her contact during office hours at the British Museum and talk about possibilities? This is exactly what happened, and, of course, a placement was offered and very successfully completed. Helen had not seen her networking opportunity at all and felt that each of the different parts of her life were separate. If you are a good networker, you can see connections and use them to everyone's advantage, including your own.

In fact, everyone you know and all their contacts can form your own networks. As you return to the world outside your kitchen, your contacts will grow in number and you will also become a greater part of other people's networks, so that it becomes a reciprocal arrangement, where you help others and they help you.

The list above is by no means exhaustive and you will, no doubt, be able to think of many other ways that you could find work. It is intended to stimulate you into thinking about your own situation and contacts and how you might be able to make the most of them to find a job that you would like.

It is, however, important to be able to recognise an opportunity when you see it, as it may come disguised or not be what you had in mind. The story below, although originally intended for a religious audience, has relevance to the area of job seeking.

> *Legend tells of a devout man who was caught in a torrential rainstorm and climbed a tree to escape the floodwaters. While the tide raged and neighbours fled, the man prayed, giving thanks for divine bounty and voicing confidence that he would be saved. As the waters rose to treetop level, a*

man approached in a rowboat and urged the praying man to climb aboard. 'No thanks,' he replied. 'My faith is strong. God will save me.' As the waters reached his chin, a helicopter lowered a rope. 'Go away,' the man shouted. 'My trust is in God.' Finally, he drowned. Coming before the heavenly seat of judgment, he vented his rage at the Almighty. 'Why did You not save me, Your faithful servant?' he cried.

'What did you want?' the Almighty shot back. 'I sent you a rowboat and a helicopter . . .'

Be sure that you are not waiting for something that, in fact, has already arrived and you just haven't noticed!

Here are lists of newspapers and their related websites, showing which jobs they advertise on which day of the week. It is as well to check this as schedules do change.

Daily Telegraph – www.appointments-plus.com
Financial Times – http://ftcareerpoint.ft.com/ftcareerpoint
Guardian – www.jobs.guardian.co.uk
Independent – www.londoncareers.net
London Jobs: *www.londonjobs.co.uk*
The Times – www.thetimes-appointments.co.uk
Yahoo job website: *http://uk.careers.yahoo.com*

TYPE OF WORK	MON	TUE	WED	THU	FRI	SAT/SUN
Accountancy	FT (up to £45k)	ES	Ind	FT (over £45k)		Ind (Sun)
Building/ Construction	ES	ES	ES		ES	
Education	ES	D Exp Gd		D Exp Ti	TES THES	S Ti
Information Technology/ Engineering		D Exp		D Exp	ES Gd	
Finance/ Banking	FT	ES		FT Ind		Ind

TYPE OF WORK	MON	TUE	WED	THU	FRI	SAT/SUN
General	ES	ES	ES FT Ind	D Exp DM D Tel (all Thu jobs repeated Sunday) ES Ind Ti	ES	D Exp Gd (Sat) Ind Obs S Ti S Tel
Legal		Ti	Ind			
Management				D Tel Ti		S Tel
Media/ Creative	Gd		ES	D Exp	Ti	
Medical/ Health	ES				Gd	
Public Sector	ES	Ti	Gd	D Exp Ind		
Sales & Marketing	Gd	ES		ES		
Secretarial	ES Gd	ES	Ti		Ti	

Key:
D Exp – *Daily Express*
DM – *Daily Mail*
D Tel – *Daily Telegraph*
ES – *Evening Standard* (London only)
FT – *Financial Times*
Gd – *Guardian*
Ind – *Independent*
Obs – *Observer*
S Tel – *Sunday Telegraph*
S Ti – *Sunday Times*
Ti – *Times*
TES – *Times Educational Supplement*
THES – *Times Higher Education Supplement*

4

Assessing your skills and the untapped resource

'Minds are like parachutes; they work best when open.'
– Lord Thomas Dewar

Assessing your skills is a necessary preparation for writing your CV and something that women often find very difficult. You need to know what your skills and strengths are in order to prepare a realistic CV.

At a time when **what** you can offer an employer, rather than **where** you have worked, is becoming more and more important, **you** are your career's greatest asset, not a list of previous employers. So finding out what your skills are and how best to market them to a prospective employer is vital – and it is important that those who have been out of the workplace for a while are able to focus on what they can do and not emphasise what they can't do. The most important part of assessing your skills when you have not been in paid work for some time is to find out what are your transferable skills.

TRANSFERABLE SKILLS

These are skills you have gained through any aspect of your life – not just your working life, but also any voluntary work you may have done, any projects undertaken for yourself or others, through being a parent, from your hobbies or sports – in fact anything that you might have perceived at the time as being a learning experience. The fact that these skills may not yet have been used in the workplace, or that someone has not paid you to use them, is irrelevant. They form part of you and your skills-set and as such can be transferred to any environment.

These lists will form the beginnings of your analysis of your skills-set and your personal strengths as well. They will need to be refined and honed to form the basis of the new CV that will market you effectively to a prospective employer.

Finding out your transferable skills, or any other kind of skills or strengths, can take time, and many women who have been out of work for a while are not sure where to start. It is also true that skills which are second nature are often not identified or even valued, so it is important that you take time and have an in-depth look at yourself.

You could begin by looking back over the years and seeing what you have done, for example:

- At home
- For the school
- Within your church or other religious community
- In a sports environment
- For a charity committee
- Helping out a friend's business
- Writing for a local magazine or newsletter

All these types of activities give you skills. You may need to sit down and itemise what you have done and then list the skills required to do these tasks well. If they were not done well, you might need to see what you should acquire to improve your skills-set – no-one is perfect and my experience of women in such situations is that they tend to be very hard on themselves when trying to assess what they are good at.

A well-known outplacement consultant came to talk to one of my groups about applying for jobs. (Organisations provide outplacement consultants to help staff whom they have made redundant to find other work.) He told us that if ten criteria were listed for an advertised job and a man had seven of them, he would be willing to 'have a go'. If a woman had eight, she would say, 'No, I can't apply for that job, I can't satisfy two of their criteria.' This seems to me a gender thing and all the groups I have worked with have borne this out. Women are their own severest critics and are less likely to have the confidence to 'go for it' than men.

Unilever has produced a sheet called 'A Mum's CV' which I reprint here with permission of Linda Emery, Head of Diversity in their London head office. They have taken a great deal of time and trouble to analyse what it is that returners have to offer and how these skills can be marketed to an employer. See what they have to say and how you may be able to refer some of the information to your own situation, even if you do not have children, to get you thinking about your own skills as preparation for your CV.

A Mum's CV
Produced by Unilever

Why is a 'Mum's CV' needed?
As a 'stay-at-home mum or dad', you acquire a wide range of new skills and competencies, which in many cases are highly similar to those needed in the workplace. However, these skills are generally unrealised and undervalued by mums themselves, and certainly by society and business. Consequently, many mothers wishing to return to work suffer a crisis of confidence, which then affects their ability to be selected for jobs. Moreover, many recruiting managers do not appreciate the skills which have been gained whilst looking after a family at home.

This document aims to help you identify the skills and competencies you may have acquired whilst looking after a family at home – and to express them in language that will be familiar to those in business.

Yes – but what about IT skills?
Potential women returners are often concerned that they do not possess the necessary IT skills to be successful in the modern workplace. Even after a break of just a few years, new IT systems may have been installed and new programmes are likely to be in use. However, most managers would accept that, provided a job-holder is of a reasonable level of intelligence, IT skills can be taught fairly easily. It is rare for the performance of a jobholder to be found unacceptable, or for promotion to be refused, because someone cannot operate the required IT systems. Think how quickly your children mastered the use of a keyboard!

There are countless other skills and competencies which are far harder to teach and which are particularly sought after in the modern workforce, notably in the area of people skills, but also things like project planning, creativity and so on.

So, how does this 'Mum's CV' work?

You will find attached a list of skills and competencies, all of which could be acquired by parents in the years they choose to stay at home to look after their children.

Each one is followed by a series of questions to stimulate thought and provide suggestions for examples of when you might have put this skill into practice. They will not all be things you have had to do – your own experience will vary enormously depending upon things like the age of your children, your family circumstances, your interests and so on. You will probably think of other examples that are unique to you.

When applying for a job you may wish to use some of these examples on your application form or CV and you will almost certainly wish to talk about them at an interview.

They should help you and others to realise that bringing up children is the best learning and developmental experience ever invented!

A Mum's CV

1. *Time management & prioritisation*
   - *Have you learnt to balance the needs of different individuals in the household (possibly allocating time to different children, partners, friends, etc.)?*
   - *Have you had to meet non-negotiable deadlines (e.g. school pick-up times)?*
   - *Have you had to develop routines and prioritise tasks (e.g. learning how to get out of the house in the morning with a new baby; learning how to get out of the house with a new baby and get an older child to school and get the house clean and do the shopping and look after an elderly relative and walk the dog and – the list could go on and on!)*

2. *Coaching and listening*
   - *Have you tried to explain the ways of the world to a small child?*
   - *Have you listened to your child learning to read and tried to help them?*
   - *Have you coached patiently as your child tried to make a birthday card for their grandmother?*

- *Have you acted as a listening ear for friends in distress and helped them see a way through their situation (or just supported them by listening)?*

3. *Creativity*
   - *Have you had to turn your hand to making costumes for school plays, designing scenery, making posters, setting up stalls for school fetes?*
   - *Have you had to come up with ideas for fundraising?*
   - *Have you had to invent games to entertain children on a rainy day?*

4. *Communication and influencing skills*
   - *Have you had to break into a whole new social set (such as building or joining networks of other mums)?*
   - *Have you put forward ideas for new ventures (e.g. new fundraising ideas for the playgroup, or Christmas lunch for other mums at the playgroup) and had to persuade others of their potential?*
   - *Have you had to plan and carry out difficult conversations with teachers when your child is unhappy or you feel the school/nursery is not acting effectively?*
   - *Have you joined any committees and voiced your point of view in a group?*
   - *Have you approached any businesses or individuals to ask for support for your school/playgroup/charity?*

5. *Project planning and organising*
   - *Have you organised a children's party (can involve planning the event, getting quotes, booking a venue and possibly entertainers, sending out invitations, keeping a tally of who is coming, preparing food, prizes, party bags, managing the event on the day. . .)?*
   - *Have you organised any events for school or nursery?*

6. *Financial management*
   - *Have you managed the household budget or part of it? Very often, having children will result in a drop in income and a rise in potential expenditure, which will require very careful budget management*
   - *Have you had to get quotes and choose suppliers for capital projects (e.g. building work, double-glazing, moving house)?*
   - *Have you had to organise a major event to a budget, such as a wedding, party or school event?*

7. *Application of IT*
   - *Have you used the Internet whilst at home? Have you tried any home shopping?*

- *Have you improved your speed of computer use by playing computer games with your children?*

8. *Crisis management*
   - *Have you had to decide instantly what to do with an injured or sick child?*
   - *Have you had to deal with insurance companies, builders or neighbours following storm damage to your house, a car crash or other catastrophe?*

9. *People management*
   - *Have you helped at school or nursery and co-ordinated the activities of other helpers or staff?*
   - *Have you run committees of volunteers or chaired meetings?*

10. *Learning new skills*
    - *Have you had to learn new skills to try and stay one step ahead of your children (whether it's to help an older child learning Russian, German or trigonometry, or to explain the LBW rule or the off-side trap used by Arsenal!)?*

To help you further with your personal skills analysis, below is a skills list, entitled 'Word Power'. Usefully, the skills are grouped under headings, making it easier for you to use them in your CV.

Word Power (reproduced with permission of St Francis Xavier University, Nova Scotia, Canada)

General purpose

A need to excel	Excellent work habits	Professional attitude
Aptitude for	Get along well with	Self-confident
Competitive drive	people	Self-disciplined
Conscientious	Good back-up for . . .	Self-reliant
Courage of	Good listener	Tactful
convictions	Keen sense of urgency	Take nothing for
Diplomatic	Mildly aggressive	granted
Discreet	Necessary ingredients	Thrive in an
Enjoy getting involved	for . . .	environment that . . .
with . . .	Persuasive	Understands priorities

Management Ability

Ability to inspire others	Decision maker	People-handling skills
Administered	Developed	Strong leader
Authority over . . .	subordinates	Successful with people
Closely supervised	Headed . . .	Took charge
Command respect	In charge of . . .	Willing to take the
Co-ordinator	Leadership ability	initiative

Competence

Ability to make	Cut out for . . .	Practical approach
practical . . .	Decisions	to . . .
Ability to see overall	Effective	Pre-plan everything
picture	Inspire confidence	Proficient
Adept at . . .	Integrity and drive	Strength in . . .
Aggressive, tactful,	Keep up with	Technical competence
and results-orientated	current . . .	in . . .
Aptitude for . . .	Know-how	Think and act maturely
Capable of	Like to find a better	Thorough
formulating and	way of doing	understanding of
directing	Like to make things	Thoroughly trained
Comprehensive	happen	Want to get involved
knowledge	Mastered	
Creative	Performance-orientated	

Intelligence

Ability to think	Fast thinking	Mental capacity
analytically	Good memory	Perceptive
Common sense	Ideas person	Probing mind
Creative	Logical thinker	

Ability to handle details

Accurate	Follow through	Perfectionist
Adept with figures	Get things done	Precise
Careful	Like details	Systematic
Detail-minded	Meet all due dates	Take pride in work
Efficient	Methodical	Well organised
Excellent memory	Orderly	
Fastidious	Pay attention to detail	

Profit orientated

Ability to trim costs and increase . . .	Eliminated bottlenecks	Reduce excessive costs
Able to identify and solve problems	Expense-minded	Relieve paperwork jams
Controlled spiralling costs	Generated cost savings	Results-orientated
Cost-orientated	Get reliable information quickly	Set priorities
Curtailed spending	Initiated profit-making . . .	Set up profit centres
Drastically cut without reducing sales	Knack for saving money	Short cut to . . .
Efficiency	Plans	Simplified procedures
Efficient	Problem solver	Streamlined
	Profit-minded	Tough on controls

Responsibility

Accelerated	Established	Revamped
Altered	Expedited	Shape and direct
Automated	Fashioned	Solid foundation in . . .
Comprehensive	Generated	Sound overview of . . .
Concentrated on . . .	Guided	Sparked
Controlled	Heavily involved in . . .	Streamlined
Coordinated	Initiated	Strong dedication to . . .
Created	Installed	Well versed in . . .
Demonstrated	Originated	
Devised	Prime emphasis on . . .	

Positive Impact

Accelerated	Generated	Reduced
Actively	Guided	Reinforced
Adapted	Implemented	Reorganised
Administered	Improved	Responsibilities
Approved	Increased	Responsible
Completed	Influenced	Revamped
Conceived	Interpreted	Reviewed
Conducted	Launched	Revised
Conferred	Led	Scheduled
Created	Maintained	Set up
Delegated	Participated	Significantly
Demonstrated	Performed	Simplified
Developed	Pinpointed	Solved
Directed	Planned	Strategy
Effected	Proficient at . . .	Streamlined
Eliminated	Programmed	Strengthened
Established	Proposed	Successfully
Expanded	Provided	Tied together
Expedited	Recommended	Triggered

WHAT STRENGTHS AND SKILLS ARE EMPLOYERS LOOKING FOR WHEN THEY RECRUIT?

My definition of a strength is a character or personality trait (e.g. reliability), and a skill is something that you have learned (e.g. fluent French).

Personal strengths that any employer would value:

Adaptability
Commitment
Common-sense
Dedication
Emotional intelligence
Enthusiasm

Flexibility
Initiative
Reliability
Self-motivation
Delivering what you say you will
Contributing to the business, adding value
Willingness to learn
Willingness to work hard

Skills that are useful in the workplace:

Ability to multi-task
Ability to work with other people and be part of a team
Budgeting
Effective time-management
Good communication skills, both written and oral
Developed interpersonal skills
Knowledge of computers and IT skills
Prioritising
Selling ability
Speaking a foreign language
Specific skills related to the business or industry of the employer

If you want to know what employers are looking for, read the advertisement pages in a newspaper and make a note of how many times a particular strength or skill is specified in different ads. This will give you an idea of what you need to be a good candidate. Look at what you have done and see how you can package your skills for a business environment. Whatever work you are applying for, there are likely to be basic requirements that all employers are looking for. Try to think of yourself as someone who is reliable and will be loyal, rather than a woman who has not worked for some years. Both viewpoints are true, but you need to focus on what you **can** offer and not the negative aspects of your career break.

THE UNTAPPED RESOURCE

What do women returners bring to the workplace that employers would value particularly? I see such women as a huge resource, the value of which employers have yet to appreciate fully.

You are less likely to move jobs frequently.
Taking on new recruits is expensive and time-consuming and an employer will want to know that you are going to give him or her a good return on that investment of both time and money. Many organisations offer training and development to all employees, not just returners, and a high staff turnover only adds to the firm's expenses. You may be looking for stability in your working life and not be keen to jump from one job to another.

You have completed your family and are not likely to leave to have more children.
This will not, of course, apply to all of you, but this viewpoint could be a big plus for those to whom it does apply. Although life can throw some unexpected surprises at us, you may feel that this is something you can push as being of extra value to an employer.

You are accustomed to working hard.
The courses we used to run at the University of Westminster included a work placement as part of their requirements. Our women used to go to an employer for four weeks, unpaid, to work on a specific project and gain some up-to-date experience. It was the ideal route back for women and so many of them returned to the course filled with astonishment at how relatively little work people did compared with what those women were used to doing at home. Most women are not afraid of hard work and will give great value for money to an employer.

You may bring diversity into an organisation.
By recruiting 'in their own image', organisations are depriving themselves of the diversity and new ideas that stimulate businesses to grow and develop. If everyone there is white, male, middle-aged and middle-class, they will all think the same and their growth will be

limited by their restricted situations. Bring women, younger people, older people, ethnic minorities, disabled people into an organisation and it benefits from all their different perspectives.

You have developed wisdom and maturity along the years.
The responsibility of being a parent, or of looking after the welfare of others, helps us to develop and grow as people with experience of life. If you have taken a career break to travel or fulfil your life's ambition, you are likely to have matured as a person and acquired skills and wisdom from that experience. We learn from all our experiences – I have certainly changed through bringing up four very different children. We learn not to panic at the first sign of a problem, we understand that there is more than one way of dealing with difficulties, we develop an awareness of other people's feelings and of controlling our own. At least, that is what I hope happens to us as we grow older and wiser! And these qualities are valuable in the workplace, where such a significant proportion of our success depends on our ability to get on with other people.

Innovative ideas developed by experience gained during time away from the world of work.
In the time spent away from the workplace, you may have gained a new perspective and experience may have given you the ability to deal more creatively with problems. Organisations can benefit greatly from the 'outsider's perspective', and you may be able to counter the arguments that 'we have always done it like this' with suggestions of more effective practice from your fresh viewpoint.

COMMON SENSE

This basic commodity is much valued in the workplace. A good dollop can temper the most fraught working conditions and allow for good working relationships. Knowing when it is time to get angry and when common sense dictates a better approach will be appreciated in all organisations and by all employers.

Yes, of course you will feel out of touch and may need some training to get you up to speed. But training is given to many people when they start at work, not just those who have been out of the workplace. So try not to focus on that negative aspect.

If you really feel after reading this chapter that you have very few skills to offer an employer, then perhaps this is the time to take a course or work as a volunteer to gain some more up-to-date experience, so that you feel you do have something to write on your CV or application form. A work placement is an excellent way of learning, without obligation on either side, but it is difficult to get one on your own. Writing to an employer and asking for some unpaid work placement (rather like school leavers who do 'work experience') is not likely to result in an offer and it is much easier to secure one as part of a course, with the strength of the course provider behind you.

Having said that, it still might be worth approaching people you know to see whether they will let you sit in at work to appreciate what goes on there. It may well de-mystify the workplace for those of you who feel it is a foreign land. And many women have told me that they do feel just that.

Case Study: Sandra

Sandra had given up working as a receptionist in the advertising industry and looked after her two daughters as a full-time mother. As her daughters grew up and became more independent, she needed to care for her mother who became very demanding when she developed Alzheimer's disease. Sandra gave up all hope of developing herself with her very time-consuming family commitments. Wanting to do something for herself, she eventually attended a course for returners after her mother had gone into residential care as the disease had progressed significantly. Sandra's personal confidence was very low and she did not know what her skills were.

After the course, she volunteered to join a local advocacy unit, where she would receive training in how to speak for others who either did not speak English or were lacking the education to do so for themselves. The training gave a huge boost to her confidence levels. She decided to take a course in social care with the aim of becoming a social worker. She was also more able to ask for help in her personal life, especially where her mother was concerned, and became less afraid of the difficulties she was facing.

The volunteering and opportunity to stretch herself mentally in a non-paid environment helped her to find a path for a future career. She wrote: 'I understand now that I am worthy of learning and am not on the scrap heap but have so much to give to others. I now have the courage to follow my dream!'

While you are at the stage of looking at your skills you will probably also be thinking about exactly what type of work you can do. This will depend on a great many factors, but let us just explore this area for a short while.

Do you want to do what you were doing before you took a career break? If you are returning to work after maternity leave, to the same position as before, you may need a brief updating session. (See the directory at the end of this book for organisations which give information on maternity rights, etc.)

If you had a career (for example, as a nurse, teacher, radiographer, social worker, PA [personal assistant], engineer), you may want to pick it up again. If you have a professional association, many of them now run refresher or updating courses for members who have left and need practical help to rejoin their profession. You may want to contact your previous employer to say that you would like a chat and see what possibilities there are for you. A short work placement or gentle intro-duction back to work may be all you need to bring you up to speed.

If you did not have a career as such, but were just working with no specific path in mind, you may find that the time out of work has given you different skills, and a new perspective on your own abilities or aspirations. You may now want to work for an organisation where you feel that you are putting something back into the community rather than one where profitability is the main focus. You will have changed from time out of the workplace and this preparation stage for returning to work is the ideal opportunity for you to assess not only what your skills are but what your values are. Ask yourself whether you would work for an organisation whose ideals you do not support (for example, a tobacco company or one that is known to exploit develop-ing countries). Think about what is important to you now and see how that fits in with the skills you have already identified.

This book cannot cover career advice as such, but there are some very useful exercises in the book by Richard Bolles, *What Color is Your*

Parachute?, to help you assess what you would like to do in terms of work. You might consult a career consultant for an individual assessment. Psychometric or aptitude testing is sometimes used and you may be provided with a list of possible jobs or careers which would suit your skills and personality type. This is, of course, quite an expensive approach but you may think it a worthwhile investment in your future career if it gives you a focus when you have none.

A book on our reading list, originally intended for school leavers, *Occupations 2004* lists every type of occupation in the UK, together with the qualifications and skills required. There is also information on professional bodies within each occupation and how to progress in that field. It is very useful, with groupings for different areas and skills. You should find it in your local library (it is quite expensive) and it is worth a read if you are floundering.

Some universities have career guidance departments which are open to more mature graduates as well as recent ones. You can get excellent advice at a reasonable cost there. There may also be career advice given at your local adult education college and even the library may have some useful addresses.

If you do not want to do what you were doing before, you may be thinking about turning a hobby into a new career. One of my course participants loves ironing and decided to work for an ironing agency that had sprung up to help the large numbers of working women in her area. If you are great at make-up, you might want to retrain as a beauty therapist or turn a talent for cake-making or photography into a new direction.

Case Study: Felicity

Felicity had given up work when her clerical post at a bank was abolished and she was made redundant. She and her husband had no children but she did have some responsibility for elder care. She had left school with few or no formal qualifications and her confidence levels were very low. It was her perception that only people with certificates would get on well and on her own admission she 'can't do exams'.

While thinking about what to do, she knew she did not want to work in an office and took a position in a garden centre as a telephonist; she was also working on her own garden, which was a real passion. She eventually decided that her long-term plan was to open her own garden centre but that she needed some experience before she was ready to do so. She targeted a local garden centre and asked whether she could gain some work experience without pay. Her hope is that they will keep her on in a paid role and she will fill in the gaps in her knowledge and gain some business experience. Later on she will start her own garden centre. Her confidence was significantly improved and she now feels able to obtain a qualification in garden management.

Once you have taken the time to look at your own skills and assess your personal strengths, you will have the beginnings of your 'core' CV which you can adapt for different applications and expand on as you gain more work experience and/or skills.

In the next chapter, we look at writing your CV with this preparation already completed.

5

CV writing

'Opportunities are usually disguised as hard work, so most people don't recognise them.' – Ann Landers

Writing a CV can be very difficult for someone who has not been at work for a while – and may seem even more difficult when that person does not know what her skills are, or what she is good at, has no idea of what she would like to do, and when her confidence is at rock bottom after a long period out of the workplace. If this describes you, read on, as there are strategies and techniques that should help rid you of the gremlins inside your head telling you any or all of the above. You can then start to believe that it is possible to come up with a CV that does you justice and achieves its aim.

And what is the purpose of a CV? It is *not* to get you a job – it is highly unlikely that you will send your CV to someone and they will offer you a job purely on the strength of what they see of you on paper. **The purpose of the CV is to get you an interview** – the opportunity to impress a prospective employer face-to-face and build on the interest in you that he/she will have gained from reading your CV.

As such, it is mainly a selling document – selling *you* and your skills. But before you can begin to produce this selling document, you need to know what your skills are. So many women have told me when we start to talk about what to put in the CV that they feel they do not have any skills at all from being at home, either from looking after their children, or from just being out of the workplace. The previous chapter on assessing your skills should have got you thinking about what you can say about yourself on your CV.

65

At this point I want to say that there is no such thing as the definitive CV that will always get you an interview, and no-one can guarantee that one particular style will work over another. There are many different ways of conveying the same information and it is really important that you feel comfortable with what is written about you in your CV. People who have been to CV-writing agencies have told me that they have come out with something that 'does not feel like me'. As *you* are the person who will have to talk about yourself from this CV, should it get you an interview, it is vital that you are comfortable with what it says and how it represents you. It may build a little on a skill to 'talk it up' – everyone does that when they are trying to make themselves sound like the ideal candidate – but do not write anything that is not true or that you are not happy to talk about at interview. You must be prepared for an interviewer to ask you about anything which you have included in your CV.

With CV writing, one size does not fit all. You should have a core CV saved on your computer to form the basis of what you use for each application. It is important that the reader feels that you have prepared your CV just for this application, rather than have an impression that it has been 'churned out' as one of many, all the same as each other. By preparing words and phrases about yourself which you can use as a 'pick and mix', you can personalise and individualise your CV for each application, and this will stand you in good stead. Because of this, it is very important that you keep a copy of what you have sent, especially if the differences in your versions are slight.

Under what circumstances will you be sending your CV?

- ❖ The most likely reason is a response to an advertisement for a specific job
- ❖ You might also send it with a speculative letter when there is no job advertised and you are asking whether there are any vacancies
- ❖ You may be sending it following an introduction from a third party (via networking) who may have put in a good word for you with a friend or colleague

❖ It may form part of a pack which you are sending to an employment agency for them to forward to prospective employers

❖ You might also be including a CV if you are starting your own business and are applying to a bank for finance. In this case it will be used to reassure the bank about your background in order to persuade them to provide finance to start up or progress your business

Before starting to write a single word of the CV, an inventory of skills should be made to see what exactly you can do, or have done and can transfer to another environment (see chapter 4 on assessing your skills).

Perhaps you are groaning now at the thought of all this preparation – I have seen eyes glaze over when I start to talk about the effort required to produce a CV that you are happy to send out. Yes, it is difficult and should be done with as much enthusiasm as you can muster, as it is in many ways the most important part of the process. It might become a little easier if you do it with a friend, or even a group, either formal or informal. Ideas can be gained by talking to other people and you may well hear them speak about what they have done and realise that this could apply to you as well. It is surprising how much we forget about what we have done over the years and it can take a while for everything to re-surface.

THE CV ITSELF

Let us take a short time to look at some very basic information about the look of your CV. Forgive me if it all sounds too obvious to you, but many women have commented that they would not have thought of some of the things I am going to mention now, and even if you know them all, they are worth ticking off your checklist when you come to prepare a finished version.

• Use the best-quality paper you can afford. Paper used for photocopying is not going to give a good impression of you. The first thing that happens when someone wants to read your CV is that they pick it up and hold it in their hand. It should have a good feel to it, be on paper which is substantial. Copy paper has a weight of 80 grams and I suggest that you use a higher grade, perhaps 90 or 100 grams, but not so stiff that it becomes card. The colour should be white or near white for ordinary applications. There are some industries where brightly coloured paper might be an asset (design or creative come to mind), but generally be conservative at this stage.

• When posting the CV, please do not fold it. You have, hopefully, gone to a great deal of trouble to present it as well as possible and it should arrive in pristine condition, without any folds. This means that you should send it in an envelope large enough for A4 sheets (C4 size) to fit without any folds. I feel that the envelope should be white rather than brown, but this is a personal preference. Certainly use a first-class stamp. Some people even go to the trouble of hand-delivering their CVs or sending them recorded delivery to ensure a safe arrival.

• How long should it be? Two pages of A4 is about right. Recruiters do not want to plough through lengthy volumes of words to find the important details, but in a very brief CV (i.e. one page) you may sell yourself short. There should usually be a covering letter with your application, highlighting what you consider to be relevant for this particular job and also explaining anything which is not suitable to go in your CV. (More on the covering letter later.)

• Do not staple the pages together but use a paper clip so that the sheets may be viewed side by side. For this reason you should ensure that your name and contact details (phone number, email address) are printed at the top or bottom of the second page, in case the pages become separated. However organised people are, mistakes do happen and you want to be sure that all the pages can be attributed to you.

• How should it be written? It must be word-processed unless you are asked for handwritten responses (this means that the organisation may well be using a graphologist to analyse your handwriting). In an age when everyone is using computers and is word-processing their applications, you will stand out right away as out of date if you handwrite yours. If you are keen to give the impression of being current and on the ball, this will have the opposite effect and will create doubt in the mind of the reader. At all times, you should be demonstrating by your actions what you say you are and can do (e.g. send the CV in on time if you are declaring that you have good time-management skills; ensure that there are no mistakes if you say that you have a good eye for detail; be absolutely sure that you do not repeat yourself and always write well and fluently if you say that this is one of your special strengths). The reader will already be forming an impression of you at this very early stage – this is human nature and we need to understand it and use it to our advantage. I have heard it said that 'first impressions last' and the process of forming a view of you as a candidate will begin as soon as the envelope is held and opened.

- What font should you use? This is a very personal issue but whatever you decide, it should be easy to read. A clear font like Arial or Tahoma or Verdana (easily found under your computer's 'Format' menu) makes reading much easier and anything that helps the reader is a plus. I use Century Gothic because it matches my business notepaper and I find it a very clear, modern font. Please do steer clear of any font which looks too much like a typewriter (e.g. Courier) as it will immediately make your application look dated. `This is an example of Courier and hopefully makes the point`. Do not use a very fancy font which might be more suitable for social stationery than business.

- What size should the font be? It might be a temptation to use either a larger or smaller font depending on whether you have too little or too much to fill two pages. I suggest that a font size smaller than 10 point may be hard to read, and larger than 14 point may look as if you did not have enough to say so just wrote it bigger! You may put certain headings or other parts in a larger (or bold) font but, generally speaking, 12 point is a good size for such documents. There should also be enough white space around the words not to make the page look crowded, but not so much that the words are lost on the page. Above all, the information should be laid out so that it is easy to read and access. If the reader has to work too hard to find out about you, you will start at a disadvantage, however small, and it is better not to.

This sentence is written in 10 point. And this is in 14 point. See for yourself.

Always make a copy of *exactly* what you have sent and keep it with a copy of the covering letter and the job application, if there is one. This will help to make you feel organised, and not confuse different applications if you are making several at the same time. It is always a good idea to get someone else to proof-read what you are sending, as it is quite difficult to find your own mistakes; your eye sees what you intended and not what you wrote. The computer's spell-checker will not pick up errors that are existing words and it is vital that your CV has no typos. If you are unable to get another person to look at it, try reading it backwards (i.e. from the last word to the first) so that you are looking at the individual words and not reading the sense of it. I never cease to be amazed at how errors creep in when I am sure that there are none.

Should you write 'CV' at the top of the page, or more fully 'Curriculum Vitae'?
This is a very personal matter but I would say that it is clear what the document is from the very start and you may not need it. But if you want to put it, ensure that there are no spelling mistakes if you use the full Latin term.

What information should go on your CV?

- ➤ Your name
- ➤ Your address
- ➤ Your contact details – home phone/mobile
- ➤ Your email (if you have one)

This should be at the top of the CV, so that the reader can see right away who you are.

Some thoughts on the above, which would seem, on the face of it, the simplest of information. Please ensure that you are consistent with the use of your name. Many women prefer to work under their maiden name but have documents, bank account, etc., in their married name. This can cause confusion and is better sorted out in your head at the beginning. Some women use their middle name or some other, so that only their official documents have their given first name. This may be important if you have to prove for any reason that you are legally entitled to work in the UK, or need to give certificates or other qualifications to back up your application. If there are discrepancies, this might be something you may want to address in the covering letter.

You may be known as, or sign your letter as, a name which is a shortened form of your formal name. You might then want to start with:

Christine (Chris) Smith or Tatiana (Tanya) Brown.

It might not be immediately apparent that you are a woman if you have an unusual name that is not English in origin. Do you want to add Ms or Mrs to the CV or give that information in your covering letter? There is no hard-and-fast rule here and you must do what you are comfortable with. But never presume that the reader will know something that is not obvious, and try not to deceive deliberately, as the discrepancy will be noticed eventually and not do your application any good. I am told by ethical recruiters that they try to read a CV without knowing whether the candidate is male or female, and just see whether they are suitable for the job. I wish all employers had this level of integrity!

As far as your phone number is concerned, consider carefully when giving your mobile number – you may be called at an inopportune moment and have to switch modes to sound businesslike and organised when you may be at the checkout in the supermarket, or in the car with screaming children. You may not have your papers to hand, nor be anywhere near them, nor have a pen and paper close by to take down details of a possible interview time or date. It is well to be prepared – even if you can see on the phone's screen who is calling, you may not have time to get organised.

We now come to the issue of your date of birth. Again, I feel that there are no hard-and-fast rules and you must do what you feel comfortable with. Generally speaking, those who are a little more mature (for argument's sake, let us say over 40) may well feel that the reader of the CV might focus on their age rather than their ability to do the job. At the time of writing (late 2003), there is no legal requirement in the UK to include your date of birth on your CV. If you do decide that you would like to include it, I would not put it at the very top but perhaps at the end with other personal information. Those who are younger may take a different perspective, which I fully respect, but so many women have said to me that they are worried about being discriminated against on grounds of age that it has become an issue to be considered. The whole subject of age discrimination is under discussion as I write and may well have been resolved by the time this book has been published.

Case Study: Anthea

Anthea was trying to return to paid work after several years' running her own business and playing a significant role in the voluntary sector on many local and national committees. She came to me with her CV which needed some work on it. The first thing she had written after her name was:

Date of Birth: 18 November 1946
Age: 57

I felt that she was only drawing attention to her concerns about her age by mentioning not only her date of birth but also how old she was. (And her CV would need looking at every time she wants to send another copy out as she may have had a birthday since the last time she used it.) I suggested that if she felt strongly about including her date of birth, she add it at the end, after she had already impressed the reader with the calibre of person she was, in the hope that her age would be of less significance than her ability to do the job. By including it right at the start, it felt to me that she was apologising for her age and indicating that it was an issue for her. Her new, re-worked CV was strong on skills and experience and less apologetic about her age.

The important thing when writing your CV is to use a style, format and language which are current and up-to-date so that the reader will be able to focus on what you can do rather than how you have presented it. Your approximate age may well be revealed when your education is detailed, or by other items in the CV.

CV profiles

After the initial contact details at the top of the page, write a short profile of yourself to assist the reader with the most important facets to which you want to draw his/her attention. I feel that this is very important and requires some skill and care in putting together. Profiles can focus on your personal qualities, or what you are looking for, or sometimes what you have done. I give some examples with comments to give you an idea of the styles possible.

How long should the profile be? Probably not more than three or four lines, perhaps in a bold typeface or in a box to make it stand out, maybe in italics or a different font from the rest (but do be careful not to use too many fonts on your CV as this will make it hard to read and look a mess). Some people preface the profile with 'Profile' or 'Personal Statement', which is fine. It should generally be written in the third person, not the first person (i.e. as if you are writing about someone else, and not by writing 'I'). This is a difficult concept to explain without a lengthy discourse into English grammar, for which there is no room now. If you read the sample profiles you will get a feel for how to express yourself in the third person. (Imagine that you are saying 'She is . . .' or 'She has . . .' and omit those two words of introduction, just writing what would come next.) The way you write should be consistent, meaning use the same part of the verb each time and do not mix parts of speech. The profile may need to be adapted for different applications, as you may need to shift the emphasis according to the type of position you are applying for.

Here are some suggestions for profiles to give you an idea of different styles. At all times the profile should be the showcase, as it were, for the best of what you can bring to an employer. It should focus more on the employer's needs than on your wants. When the employer reads it, the ideal response would be, 'I must find out more about this person, she sounds interesting, as though she may have something we are looking for'. The response you do not want is 'Well, I can see what *she* wants but what about *our* needs?'

• *An organised and professional qualified educational psychologist seeking to gain experience in her profession. Willing to undertake any continuous professional development necessary, committed to children's development and highly motivated to make an impact in her chosen profession.*
(This woman has a profession but no experience. She would like to gain some up-to-date experience in her chosen field.)

• *Conscientious and reliable school administrator with well-developed people skills. Sympathetic and organised with significant experience in a school environment and able to use own initiative.*
(This woman knows what she is looking for – she wants to work in a school environment, though she may have gained her administrative experience in another field. What is important is that she can give evidence of it.)

• *An articulate and experienced individual, able to relate to people at all levels, having significant expertise with action groups and the voluntary sector. Able to motivate others and inspire both confidence and trust through excellent communication skills, combined with intelligence and integrity.*
(This woman has a great deal of experience in the voluntary sector and wants to transfer those skills to paid employment. She is focusing on her personal qualities as she does not really know what she could do.)

• *A caring and reliable individual who is willing to work hard, having gained experience working with children in the classroom. Has well-developed communication and listening skills. Would be willing to undertake any training necessary to further increase knowledge and understanding.*
(This woman has also gained some experience as a volunteer classroom assistant and now wants to work in a paid role, building on her experience. She also realises that she may need more training.)

• *Hardworking individual, with over 10 years' work experience in banking. Recently moved to the UK and therefore seeking a position that will utilise existing skills, experience and qualifications. Willing to undertake any necessary training.*
(This woman wants to return to her previous career in banking after time abroad but knows, after a break, that she may need updating. She also is emphasising her personal qualities.)

• *An articulate and enthusiastic individual with strong interpersonal and organisational skills combined with a high degree of reliability and integrity. Works efficiently and accurately, particularly under pressure. Has adapted to an ever-changing living and working environment, mixing with different cultures and backgrounds.*
(This woman has spent some time living abroad in different countries. She is turning the disadvantage of being out of the employment market in the UK into an advantage, by emphasising what she has gained by living and working abroad, and the fact that she can manage and adapt to frequent change. An employer will value this easily transferable skill.)

These profiles are just random examples of real women returners to give you an idea of length and style. They are not intended for you to copy completely as each one is so individual – rather like fingerprints. There are similarities but you need to find your own, unique version.

Rather than a profile of you, you may prefer to use a career objective at the top of your CV. This is better for those who are more focused and may look something like this:

• *Objective: To achieve a career in publishing where my hard work is valued, my talent admired, my experience used, my dedication and loyalty acknowledged and my honesty rewarded.*
(This has been used in the first person as it has a stronger feel to it – as I have said before, there are no hard-and-fast rules.)

• *Career objective: Seeking to make a contribution to the workplace with highly developed interpersonal and time-management skills gained in the voluntary sector. Greatly motivated to work to the highest possible standards at all times to add value to an organisation.*

(This woman makes it clear that she is returning to paid work but focuses on what she has to offer. The objective, although personal, still needs to present the candidate from the employer's perspective; i.e. what she can bring rather than what she wants.)

Once you are happy with your profile or objective, what comes next? Basic information included in your CV should cover:

❖ Your education and qualifications, including any training you have received
❖ Your employment history or work experience (most recent first)
❖ Your main skills and achievements, where relevant
❖ Your hobbies and interests
❖ Any personal details you want to reveal
❖ A brief statement about references

The order in which this information will be set out depends on the application, your background and the style of CV which you choose to use.

THE STYLE OF CV

There are two basic formats for the body of the CV (with several variations), but they can be classified as **chronological** or **skills-based** (sometimes called **functional**). My impression is that with so many people being out of the workforce for such a wide range of reasons (redundancy, children, travelling, sabbaticals, caring for elderly relatives, ill-health, to name but a few) the skills-based CV is becoming much more usual, as it does not focus on where you have worked, so that gaps are not so evident, but rather looks at the candidate and what she has to offer, which is a plus for women who have been out of work and are not sure how to manage the gap. There is also an issue in that many organisations which you may have been proud to display on your CV have fallen out of favour and where you worked may no longer be as prestigious as you thought. Some of them may not even exist any longer! What you can offer and your skills-set are becoming increasingly more important.

However, if you are seeking to return to the field in which you worked before, or even to the same organisation, a chronological CV may suit you better. If not, and especially if you are looking to work in a completely new direction, the skills-based CV may be more appropriate.

After your personal profile, some headings are useful to organise the information you are presenting to the reader.

The Chronological CV

If you are opting for a chronological CV, the logical information to put next is your career/employment history, always starting with the most recent first. Where you worked in 1977 will be of little interest; the last few years are probably the most relevant. Try not to use abbreviations that are not easily understood, or use them in full the first time – Ernst and Young (E&Y). The reader does not want to feel excluded at any time from sharing this information or stupid for not knowing what to you is obvious. Either way you will not endear yourself to them. (For a quick guide to some commonly used abbreviations look in the reference section at the end of this book.) Some people like to list a few key tasks, responsibilities and/or achievements within each job listed, to expand a little. This is fine but try to avoid repetition and use strong words in terms of achievements.

Under **Employment history**, you might put sub-headings:

Position: Job title or description of the type of work you have done.

Responsibilities: A short paragraph outlining the nature of the work you were involved in and information on any staff you may have supervised/managed or otherwise had responsibilities for. If it is not obvious from the name of the organisation, also mention the type of business.

Key achievements: Briefly, say how well you did the job, what you successfully achieved and how well you contributed to the team or the organisation as a whole. Include any involvement in special projects or recognition for work you did (either from customers or within the company). You could use bullet points or brief sentences for this. Try to keep it in the same style as the profile, i.e. as though you were writing about someone else.

It is very hard to give examples that will be relevant for all readers as your backgrounds and experiences will be so diverse. Here is just one example to give you an idea:

> **Employment history** (could also call this Work experience if you feel happier):
> 2000–2003
> **Position**: Conference organiser for the Citizens Advice Bureau (CAB)
> **Responsibilities**: In charge of organising and producing conferences for volunteers working in CAB offices
> **Key achievements**:
> ✓ Produced over 20 high-level, successful, well-attended conferences and training courses
> ✓ Developed and produced ground-breaking residential seminars on current legal and consumer issues
> ✓ Worked with team of volunteers from offices throughout the UK

Whether you have been paid to do this or not, it is clear that you have the skills required and those are what an employer will be looking for.

In the chronological CV, perhaps you might next list your education and qualifications, together with any training you have received.

Education, qualifications and training:

The location of the section on your education and qualifications may well depend on how relevant they are to the job you are applying for. If you are applying to be an educational psychologist, it would be very important to show early in your CV that you have the relevant qualifications and have attained the academic standard required. Should you be applying to run a restaurant, where fewer formal qualifications are required, you may feel inclined to list your education later on, and focus instead on your management and people skills.

There are no hard-and-fast rules and your CV should be adapted for each application.

For your formal schooling and education, it is usually better to start with the highest level of qualification you have reached: if you have a degree there is little point in listing all your GCSEs and their grades, unless there are some unusual ones, or you are required to show a minimum level of numeracy and literacy.

If you have very few qualifications, your CV may want to reflect what you can do or offer as a person. If you have already looked at your own skills and strengths, you will have worked out what they are. Any relevant training you have received should be included, even if it was not at work, or was in a voluntary role.

For the skills-based CV
After the profile or objective, headings are a good way of high-lighting your main skills. They might include (and will need to be varied according to your background and what you are applying for):

Organisational skills
Interpersonal and communication skills
Information technology
Financial/budgeting skills
Research skills

Each of these headings requires some information to expand on them, usually given in bullet-point format to make it easy to read and access information. For example:

- ❖ An eye for detail and a commitment to deliver the best possible outcome
- ❖ A 'can-do' attitude to getting the job done
- ❖ Set up many events from proposal to final completion
- ❖ Highly organised in office administration and the management of databases
- ❖ Effective communicator with people whether face to face or via the telephone
- ❖ An ability to build rapport and relationships with people easily
- ❖ Able to deal with difficult customers

❖ Efficient and capable researcher with a determination to search out information
❖ Persuasive and practised in managing people effectively
❖ Problem-solver when necessary
❖ Endowed with plenty of common sense and a well-developed sense of humour
❖ Experience of managing budgets and working within tight financial constraints
❖ Efficient in use of information technology, including most of the commonly used software packages

(All these come from CVs of real women returning to work. I have intentionally chosen them from a wide range of women and varied the level and complexity of what is included. They are only to give you ideas and should not be copied into your CV.)

Just a word about bullet points and their different styles. They can be simple black bullets, or round circles, but I have seen ticks used, which can be very positive in tone (I have seen the ticks in red, which is even more affirming). Never use crosses or anything that might have a negative connotation.

Examples are provided throughout this chapter. See which ones you like best.

Hobbies and interests:
Some people feel that this section has no relevance to your ability to do the job, and while I do, in principle, agree with this, when there is little to choose between two candidates, something in this section may just swing the balance in your favour. For example, a first-aider's certificate might be useful in certain lines of work; if working with children and you are a swimming life-saver, this could be very valuable. Perhaps you have some special skill or interest, outside the usual 'reading, visiting the theatre, socialising with friends' that so often appear at this point. You may want to mention sports to indicate that you are fit and well. You may have a very unusual interest which gives the impression of a very rounded and versatile person, for example, bread-making, or fencing, or even skydiving. In my opinion, it is worth mentioning.

Personal information:

What about your marital status? I do not feel that it is essential; you may want to include it and whether you have children, but I believe that it is not required, especially when it is irrelevant to your ability to do the job. I would hope that all good employers would be looking to recruit the best person for the job, and not the one who is the most convenient to employ. Some women feel strongly that they do want to mention their children, and if this is you, then say, for example: 'Three children, aged between four and ten years'.

People often mention that they have a clean and full driving licence (if they do) at this point, and it may be worth adding here, even if the job has no explicit connection with driving at all. You never know when it might become important.

References:

I would not suggest including the details of your referees on your CV as you may need to ask different people according to your application. Certainly, you should contact your proposed referee *before* you give the prospective employer details, as you want to ensure that:

- They are not going on holiday/into hospital at the time you will need them to give you a reference
- They are not so busy that they will not have time to do it
- They have no vested interest in the organisation or find that there is a conflict of interest and they are unable to do it
- They may not want to provide a reference for any reason which they do not need to tell you

Usually a reference is given by a previous employer, but as you may find this difficult after a long break, these people may be worth approaching if they know you well enough:

- Your doctor
- A solicitor
- A magistrate
- A course tutor
- The Chair of a voluntary association you belong to
- A town councillor

➤ A friend who is a personnel officer
➤ Your religious minister

Your referee ordinarily will have known you for more than two years, but I have given many references for course participants whom I have known for considerably less. In the written reference I have stated in what capacity I know the candidate and for how long. To my knowledge, this has never been a problem.

Generally speaking, references are only taken up when the employer is ready to offer the job, which may be given 'subject to references' – so the referee will know what stage your application has reached. Time may be of the essence, so choose someone you know to be reliable in this matter. It does happen that referees do not, in the end, want to give a reference and if they are late in sending it back, the employer may have drawn an inference about your character or situation which might not be correct. It is also true that employers are not always as organised time-wise as they should be, and I have received many requests which give very little time to prepare a thorough reference. Usually, details of the relevant job are supplied so that the referee can properly assess the candidate's suitability.

Writing your CV should take some time and may be a 'work in progress' – as you gain experience or knowledge you may need to update it, or change its focus slightly if you decide to apply for something different. That is how it should be – it is never totally complete if you are growing and developing as a person and acquiring new skills. If you have created a CV that does you justice, then you might be called for an interview, and it will have done its job.

If you are asked to complete an application form rather than submitting a CV, the following chapter deals with how to complete the form effectively, together with guidance on the covering letter.

6

The application form and covering letter

'There is a very real relationship, both quantitatively and qualitatively, between what you contribute and what you get out of this world.' – Oscar Hammerstein II

What about the application form? You may be poised to send your carefully crafted CV and find that you are sent an application form to complete. Many women have told me that they feel totally daunted at the prospect of this; many go no further with their application as they cannot fill in the form. Let us take a moment to look at the form more closely and see how to do it.

First of all, you should always make a copy (or two) of the form and put away the original until you are ready to write on it and send it in. This will take away the pressure to do it perfectly as you have a copy to practise on and the original to make more copies from, should you need to.

Before starting to fill in the form, read it all the way through a couple of times to see what they are looking for and what is required to fill it in. Do they want block letters, black ink, information that you do not have readily to hand? Prepare yourself and then look at the easiest questions, probably your **personal details**. They may want your National Insurance number (NI) – most people do not know theirs by heart so you might need to find it. (A section at the end of the book has brief details of useful information regarding financial matters.) Bear in mind, if you give your mobile number you may be contacted at awkward moments (see section on page 71 re the CV) – the form I have in front of me as I write does ask for it, as well as day and evening numbers.

If you are asked for your **date of birth**, I would strongly advise you to answer honestly. I have heard of people trying to lose a few years, especially if they look younger than they are. The problem with this approach is that if you are found out (and other questions may inadvertently reveal your true age), you will create a doubt in the reader's mind about your integrity that will be very hard to remove.

Then try to complete the section that seems the easiest for you to do – perhaps the one on **education, qualifications and training**, as you may have that information already to hand for other purposes if you are preparing with any seriousness to return to work. It is generally better to put N/A (not applicable) rather than leave blanks, which give the impression that you may have forgotten to answer. Generally, it is best to start with your highest level of education – if you have GCSEs (or 'O' Levels) as your highest formal qualification, it may be useful to put the number you have gained; grades, I feel, are not so important if they are all at or above pass level, and you may want to indicate that you have Maths and English, two basic subjects required, and any others that are of particular relevance to the job you are applying for.

If you have a first degree, or higher academic qualifications, GCSEs and 'O' Levels are of less interest to an employer unless they are particularly unusual ones, relevant to the post. You may also be asked about any professional associations you belong to. You may be a lapsed member but the connection may be relevant and possibly worth mentioning.

Under **training**, I would include anything you have done, even in a voluntary role, as this will give you skills you can demonstrate. Perhaps you have done some IT updating, received training as volunteer for a charity, been on a team-building exercise within your community, taken a course for women returners, etc.

Under **employment history**, there may be some difficulty if it is a long time since you have worked. It is important that you do not apologise for not having been in work – just state something like 'Have not been in recent employment as I have been at home raising my children/caring for my disabled mother/following a period of time abroad', and then put in a previous employer from when you were last in work, even if it was a long time ago, if it is relevant. If you do not have an employer you are happy to include, at least you have put something in this section. You may want to expand on it in your covering letter, but explain, do not apologise.

Other relevant experience may provide your chance to show that, although you have not been in paid work, you have gained skills while at home that can be transferred to the workplace. Think about your voluntary work, your hobbies, your sports and all the other elements of your life – look again at the section earlier in this book on identifying your skills. Most employers now will value skills you can demonstrate even if they have not been gained in paid work – the world of work is a much more flexible place than it used to be, and people are taking time out and returning in more significant numbers than used to be the case.

The most important part of the application form, in my opinion, and what will mark out the candidate likely to be called for interview is the **personal statement**. The employer may well have a checklist to tick off how far each candidate meets the criteria they are looking for; this will be your opportunity to shine and show that you have understood what they are looking for and can make a significant contribution to their business or organisation.

Look at some of the phrases you have thought of for your CV and see how they can be incorporated into this statement. You may be asked to continue on a separate sheet if there is not enough room, or you may prefer to take the whole section and write it on a sheet on its own. Ensure that you indicate that the separate sheet is attached. A useful strategy is to make a chart for yourself, with the criteria the employer is looking for on one side and the evidence you can give for meeting or exceeding them on the other. This will ensure that you do not miss out anything that they may be looking for when you complete the form. Remember that they will want to ask you questions about what you have written on the form, as with your CV, so ensure that you can back up what you are saying with concrete examples should you be called for interview.

A word here about how candidates are selected for interview: I am told by a regular visitor to my women returners' course, the HR manager in a local authority, that a scoring system is used by some organisations when deciding whom to interview. Candidates are listed with a number, so that their identity is not known, and the criteria the employer is looking for are enumerated, with a scoring system like the one below:

Does not meet (the criterion)   0
Partially meets   1
Meets and exceeds   2

So a completed grid (I am only using a few examples to give you an idea of how it works) might look something like this:

Criterion	Candidate No.1	No.2	No.3	No.4	No.5, etc.
Experience of budget control	0	2	2	1	1
Office experience	1	1	2	2	0
IT skills	0	2	2	2	1
Total:	1	5	6	5	2

Once this grid has been completed and totalled, it will be relatively easy to see who is suitable for interview. If the employer were hoping to interview six candidates, taking into consideration the length of time it takes to conduct interviews and the time available for doing so, then the six top-scoring candidates would be called, provided, of course, that they were suitable in all other areas. A very sensitive employer may well read other elements in the form if he/she felt that the candidate had not done themselves justice in the personal statement, but not all recruiters will work in this way.

It is important for a woman returning to work to list what she can do, even if she has not done it in a paid environment, because she will get some credit for it. For example, if you have not had experience at work of managing budgets, but have run your household on a limited amount of money and understand the principles of working within financial constraints, then say so in your personal statement as you will be given some credit for it. If you do not mention it, you will get a zero. If the employer is looking for good team-working skills and you have run the local Brownie pack, worked with others and delegated responsibilities for Brownie-pack holidays, then mention it. The information you need to know, for example, what skills you have and what you have done in your career break, should be at your fingertips if you have worked through chapter 4, or if you have completed a CV.

You will also be asked about **references**. This is often a difficult area for women who have not worked for a while, as they are not sure whom to ask. Please see what I have written earlier about referees in the chapter on CV writing, which applies equally here.

There may also be other forms with the application pack – possibly a **declaration** of criminal offences and an **equal opportunities** form. The criminal offences form usually gives details of which offences are considered 'spent' (i.e. you do not need to declare them after a certain period of time), and which are not.

Equal opportunities forms (with questions on ethnicity, marital status, age band, etc.) are usually separated from application forms as soon as they are received (they are often in lurid, bright colours to make them easy to identify) and are not seen by the people doing the shortlisting. They are for monitoring purposes only and not for discriminating. Some people prefer not to fill these in – I leave that to your own judgement.

The section on **disability** is also included to ensure both that the organisation has a sufficiently diverse workforce and that disabled candidates are not disadvantaged. Many adverts, particularly those for jobs in the public sector, now state that *'We are committed to increasing the diversity of employees at all levels, particularly the representation of people with disabilities, women and ethnic minorities in key positions'.*

When you are happy with your trial application forms, carefully copy all the information on to the one you are going to send, and then, if you wish, make a copy of that, so you have an exact record of what you have sent. As with the CV, I would not fold the form but send it, with an accompanying letter, in the best envelope you can afford, taking note of the deadline for applications.

If you have just missed the deadline, it might still be worth calling to see whether your application will be considered – there may not have been a huge response, or they may wish to see you for other reasons. It is always worth a phone call – but not months after the deadline!

Some applications are invited using an online form that is to be completed like one that you might receive in the post. People sometimes find that these forms are difficult to navigate online and prefer to print one out to complete in the traditional way. Usually the spaces included will adjust their size to your text, but it can be very frustrating if you have a longer than average name, or want to write something for which there is not enough room. The information given above on application forms is also relevant for online applications.

THE COVERING LETTER

It is usual to send a covering (or accompanying) letter with your application, whether it is by CV or application form. Writing a good letter can make a significant difference to whether you are called for interview.

Case Study: Claire

Owing to the relocation of her husband's job, Claire had been living abroad. When she returned to the UK she wanted to start a new career with an insurance group. Taking a great leap of faith, she applied for a job for which she had none of the required experience, but she wrote an exceptionally good covering letter, outlining her personal qualities and what she thought she could bring to the organisation. Her passion shone through in the letter and the prospective employer, a man of vision it would seem, decided to interview her. She turned out to be equally passionate at the interview and got the job. She learned about the business very quickly and was a great success.

It is impossible to give you a letter that will do for all applications as the range of jobs and individual women is so great. However, I reproduce below a template that will give you an idea of what to include in the letter, and the approximate length and style.

Your Address
Your telephone number

Employer's Name
Employer's Title
Name of the Organisation
Address
Post Code

Date

Dear Dr/Prof./Mr/Ms/Mrs (name of employer):

Re: Specific job title or reference number (optional)

Introductory paragraph: State why you are writing, naming the specific position for which you are applying. If you are writing a solicited letter of application, explain how you found out about the opening.

Second paragraph: Tell the employer what you can offer him/her. Demonstrate that the skills, experience and education that you possess will meet his/her needs. Use active verbs to emphasise your capabilities (e.g. planned, organised, designed – see examples in Word Power on page 54). Refer briefly to accomplishments that are relevant to the job for which you are applying. Identify at least one thing about you that is unique – that makes you the best candidate to fill the organisation's needs.

If you are answering an advert or a job request, be sure to address all the requirements the employer stipulates. For example, if he/she requires a computer language or hospital experience, indicate that you have these requirements.

Third paragraph: Explain briefly why you are interested in working for this employer. If possible, reveal some knowledge of the organisation to which you are applying; explain why this organisation and/or position interests you. Refer your reader to the attached CV; invite him/her to seek out more information about you there.

Closing paragraph: Open the door for an interview and repeat your phone number here if you wish. Thank the reader for his/her time.

Yours sincerely

(Your Signature)

Your Name
Enclosure

(Adapted from Centre for Student Employment and Career Development, St Francis Xavier University, Nova Scotia, Canada.)

I reprint here a speculative letter that produced the desired result (an interview). It too would need adapting, but gives you an idea of positive tone and language.

(Name and contact details as before)
Dear Steven

David Brown suggested I contact you. I am currently looking for new employment in conferencing, having recently moved back from New York, where I was living for six months. I have previously worked in conferences for Apex Financial and prior to that, with Zenith Conferences in London.

I noticed on your website that you are advertising for the position of Conference Programme Director and I am interested in applying for this position. Although my main area of expertise was in the financial industry, I believe that the research, conference production, marketing and event planning and organisational skills I have gained both in work and other areas of my life are transferable to other sectors.

I have attached my CV for your information and will call you in the week beginning March 1st to see whether we could meet to take this forward. Thank you for taking the time to read this letter.

Yours sincerely

Jane Roberts

It is vital that you follow up a letter like this with a call if you say you are going to – unless, of course, you have heard from the person before that. Being specific about follow-up makes you sound really organised and I prefer it to the ending that usually goes, 'I hope to hear from you soon', as it is so vague. But you may prefer it as it does not commit you to calling.

If you have filled in the application form well, or created a CV that does you justice, then you might be called for an interview. The following chapter deals with managing the next stage.

7

The interview

'You never get a second chance to make a first impression.'

When I mention the word 'interview' to groups, they usually begin to hyperventilate at the prospect of facing someone across a room and trying to sell themselves. If the process of putting together a CV feels difficult, and this is only on paper, how much more does that 'face to face' moment instil fear and terror into women who have not worked for some time.

When asked what people are most afraid of at the interview, this is what has been said:

- Not being able to answer the question and drying up
- A written test
- Being nervous and looking and acting it
- Issues to do with age
- Being under scrutiny/being judged
- Not wanting to be rejected

Many of these are concerns that anyone attending an interview would feel, but there are some that are particularly relevant to women who haven't worked for a time and whose confidence is low. I hope that as you read this chapter you will develop your own personal way of dealing with the issues that trouble you most about the interview. For me, the most important part of going to an interview is the *preparation*.

- Preparing yourself and how you look
- Preparing how to get there and for the practicalities of the interview
- Preparing with research about the organisation and whatever you can find out about the job itself
- Preparing answers to likely questions

I cannot stress enough the importance of being prepared; I never cease to be amazed at people who go for interviews without any preparation at all and wonder why they do not succeed. I cannot guarantee that you will get a job with these strategies and there are so many variables that cannot be controlled – the political situation (is the country at war or about to be?/is a general election coming soon?), the economic situation (is there a recession?/are employers looking to recruit in general?), your field (are there too many people chasing too few jobs?), where you live (are there jobs in your field near enough to where you live?) – to mention but a few. But I can tell you that if you do not prepare, you will not get what you are after. I know of a recruiter who, after ten minutes with a prospective candidate who had not prepared for the interview said, 'There is little point in carrying on this inter-view, as you have clearly not even looked at our website, let alone properly prepared for it. Let us use the remaining time to give you some feedback for future applications so that you can learn from this.'

Not all HR people are so benevolent but there is a lesson there for us all. So, let us start with the most basic part of the preparation process – *you*.

WHAT ARE YOU GOING TO WEAR?

This might sound frivolous but research that I conducted at the University of Westminster showed us that what people wear at work is very important. Just as you would try to impress someone on your first date, so should you make a special effort at the first meeting of what could be a long-standing connection between you and the employer. It is said that first impressions last, and this is especially significant at the interview stage when the first impression of you will be visual.

I suggest that it is better to dress more smartly than required rather than less smartly, as you can always 'dress down' afterwards if the organisation has a less stringent code, but you might find it harder to go the other way. We all have jeans and comfortable loose track bottoms, but this is the time to show that you can be business-like. You will also feel different when you are dressed-up, even if only a little more so than usual. For me, it is all in the shoes – if I am wearing business-like shoes, I feel more sharp and capable. I think that a jacket of some sort looks the part. Take a look at your wardrobe and see what you have that you could wear for an interview. You do not want to find that you are successful with an application and then spend ages trying to find something to wear. If you have not worked for a while, you may well have little other than casual clothes and a 'posh frock' for special occasions. I recall that when I started to think about returning, I had no idea what women wore to work; all my clothes were years out of date and made me feel dowdy and out of touch. This is an important barrier to overcome if you are conscious of your age and are trying to give the impression that your age is less important than what you can do. The process begins with what you are wearing.

This does not mean spending a great deal of money but I think that you might see one suit (with skirt or trousers or both) as an investment in your future career. If you are ready to return to work, you need to look the part at the interview stage. Trousers are acceptable in the workplace now, but steer clear of casual ones – no track bottoms or loose, elasticated leisurewear, but a tailored pair with a formal look to them will stand you in good stead. I suggest a dark basic neutral colour – black/navy/grey – that you can team with blouses/shirts/tops of different colours, whatever you are comfort-able with. It may be worth finding out whether the organisation has a dress code. Even if you are going for an interview at a children's nursery where there is likely to be no strict rule about clothes, go to the interview smartly dressed as it gives the impression that you have made an effort.

Let us talk about make-up for a moment. A little make-up gives you a groomed look and this is what you should be aiming for at the interview. Women I have trained are divided over this, but I would like each of you reading this to think about what you feel concerning make-up. The 'spread on with a trowel' look is definitely to be avoided but if you are still using the make-up and techniques you employed when you last worked in 1990, then I think the time has come for a re-vamp. Many large stores will give free advice or a make-over at their make-up counters; talk to friends who look discreetly polished and groomed; experiment with looks to find out what you are comfortable with. You have to feel good about yourself at the interview, so that you will not worry about what you look like and can concentrate on showing that you are the best candidate for the job.

Ensure that, whatever you wear:

- Your clothes are clean and fresh
- You have no ladders in your tights; if you are wearing socks, they are a pair (I speak from experience here!)
- Your hands and nails are clean and well groomed
- You do not wear lashings of extravagant perfume
- Your hair is clean and organised (you should not be fiddling with it)
- If wearing a skirt, your hemline is not too short
- Your clothes are not wearing you
- You look appropriate for the organisation you want to join
- Your make-up is discreet and subtle
- Your handbag is not so full that when you place it on the floor it empties out its contents
- You are not wearing a top that is see-through or very low-cut
- If you wear glasses, that you have them with you, especially if they are reading glasses and you do not wear them all the time
- You feel comfortable in what you are wearing
- Your style is modern and does not date you – this includes your hairstyle

These are only guidelines, of course, but this is where you should be starting to prepare yourself for the interview. Confidence comes from within and I believe that you will perform better if you are confident that you look your best.

HOW CAN I PREPARE WHEN CALLED FOR INTERVIEW?

There is quite a bit of information that you can obtain to avoid nasty surprises or disorganisation:

- Find out the exact address where you will be interviewed (in a large organisation it may not be the address you wrote to, or where the job is located)
- Ask for details of public transport or location of parking nearby (ensure you have parking money to hand on the day)
- Find out how long the interview is timed to last (even an approximate time is helpful)
- They may tell you whether there will be one interviewer or more, or even a panel – at least you will not be taken by surprise
- It may be helpful to know how many interviews there will be before they select the candidate – they should tell you this, or it may be in their information pack – ensure that you have read it
- They might, if pressed politely, tell you how many candidates they are seeing, but they might not
- You could ask about a dress code if you are unsure about what to wear (e.g. 'Are trousers for women acceptable wear in the organisation?')
- Sometimes interviews are conducted with individual candidates, sometimes in a group environment, sometimes a combination of both
- Ask if there will be written parts to the interview. If there are, see if you can get any details of what they will be (some organisations use psychometric testing and sample tests are available on the Internet)

By finding out as much as possible you can limit the unknown, which may help allay your nervousness. When you get in the room to be faced by eight people on an interview panel and you are prepared for it, you will not be thrown but say to yourself, 'Yes, I was expecting this'.

Do allow plenty of time for the journey there – it is far better to arrive early and calm down with a few relaxing moments (cup of coffee/visit to the ladies/glass of water) than to arrive late, out of breath and looking harassed. You may well have about 30 minutes to impress them with the calibre of your application and you do not want to spend the first ten minutes catching your breath and smoothing down your clothes. Most of the bullet points above are just plain common sense, but there may be one or two that you had not thought of, which will ensure that you arrive in the best possible condition for the interview.

If you are offered a drink of water, accept even if you are not thirsty. You may find your mouth a little dry from nerves later on, or you may use the drinking of the water to collect your thoughts after being asked a tough question. In that couple of seconds, an answer may come to you if you have prepared well.

Take a notepad and pen with you to the interview and ask if you may use them. This makes you look prepared; you may also have noted down some questions when, as often happens, you are asked at the end if there is anything you would like to ask the interviewers. The notebook is not for you to use as a form of 'exam crib' when asked questions, but you could include a few bullet points covering things that you particularly want to bring up in the interview and are worried about forgetting. The notebook is also useful for writing down what you were asked and how you replied when the interview is over. It is amazing how quickly we forget what we have said, and taking a few quiet minutes after the interview can be very useful later on. If you are successful, it will remind you of what you told them at the interview – if you are not successful, it can be used as a learning opportunity, especially if you are given feedback as to why you were unsuccessful. This is always worth doing: you may discover useful information about your performance and, if you are receptive to learning, it will help you for the future. Also take with you any paperwork connected with this application, especially the exact version of your CV that you sent in and anything which they sent you. Putting it in a folder or plastic pocket makes you look organised and efficient. Having their phone number with you means that you can contact them if you are unavoidably delayed.

Case Study: Delia
Delia had an interview and heard that she was not successful after getting down to the last two. As she was keen to find out why she had

*not got the job, she called the organisation and asked for feedback on
her performance. They were very impressed with her, they said, but
there had been a candidate with exactly the qualities and experience
that they were looking for. However, they were so interested in her
and the fact that she had called for feedback, that they offered her a
job. Although slightly different to the one that she had applied for, she
was thrilled to accept it.*

A word here about body language. I do not profess to be an expert in
this area, but I do know that body language can reveal how we are
feeling and send out powerful signals. If I am talking to someone and
there is a discrepancy between what they are saying and their body
language, I am more likely to take notice of the non-verbal signal than
what they are saying. I believe this to be true about everyone. Just try
to say something sweet and gentle to someone using a harsh tone of
voice with your arms crossed confrontationally – you will never
convince them that you mean what you are saying in the face of
conflicting body language. Think of your whole impact as comprising
'words and music' – the words represent the verbal part of your
communication, the music represents the non-verbal part. If they are
in harmony with each other, your message – i.e. what you are saying
– is accepted and believed. But if they are not in harmony, the listener
will believe the 'music', i.e. your non-verbal signals. Our human-
animal instincts seem to me to be programmed in this way and we are
used to trusting our instincts.

Tone of voice I take to be included in body language. When
answering questions, try not to speak too loudly or too softly. Practise
with a friend or looking in a mirror, or even talking to a tape recorder
and playing it back (some people do not recognise their own voices at
all). Consider the speed at which you are talking – when we are
nervous we tend to talk faster so you may need to slow yourself down.
On the other hand, you do not wish to talk so slowly that you give the
impression of being a slow thinker.

In terms of body language itself, walk in to the room with good
posture and look at all the people there. Smile and give a warm and
firm handshake, if appropriate, to the person who greets you. If there
is a panel, it may be rather time-consuming to shake everyone's hand,
but a brief acknowledgement with a nod of the head and a smile

would be fine. It is hard to smile when you are nervous, so practise!

Try to sit as comfortably as you can, without worrying about your clothes, fussing with your hair, fiddling with your jewellery. (See the section on page 93 on what to wear – this is why it is so important that you are comfortable in your clothes and are not thinking about your appearance at all; you need to focus on what you are saying.)

It is important to make eye-contact but not to stare in an intimidating way. Look round at the other people in the room, keeping your voice well-modulated as you answer their questions. A monotone will suggest that you are bored or not interested, which you want to avoid, and a high-pitched voice suggests anxiety. If you lean forward at times, you will give the impression of being enthusiastic and interested. Sitting back with an overly casual look can give the wrong impression and the interviewers will be *looking* at you as much as they are *listening* to what you are saying. Try not to talk too much with your hands as this can be distracting.

When it is time to go, stand up without fussing, look the interviewers warmly in the eye and extend your hand. 'Thank you for your time', or something like that, is an appropriate note on which to leave. Remember that you are being assessed from the moment you walk in to the premises until you walk out – be courteous and polite to everyone you meet from first to last. Your interviewer may ask the receptionist or doorman how you treated them; when you are leaving, ensure that you are on your best behaviour until you are out of the door. A seemingly casual comment at the door, or the lift, may still be part of the interview and you don't want to be caught off your guard. At all times appear positive and enthusiastic about this job and never criticise a previous employer or colleagues.

Of course you will be nervous; not to be would be completely abnormal. A little adrenalin, which is produced when we are nervous or excited, can give you the 'edge' needed to produce your best performance. A good interviewer will know that you are nervous and should make allowances for it at the start, but as you settle down, you should find that the butterflies subside and you can get down to the business of showing yourself in the best light.

It may happen that you are not interviewed by a competent interviewer – in an ideal world, everyone would always work to the highest standards of best practice but, as we all know, this is not an ideal world. A good interviewer will ask open questions (those which require more than a 'yes' or 'no' answer) and these questions will not usually be ambiguous. If you are not clear what is wanted, you could ask for clarification, by saying, 'I am not sure what you mean by . . . Please could you be a little more precise?' If you have not been paying attention and need a question repeated, you could say, 'Please could you repeat the question as I did not get it/understand it/hear it the first time?' But you can't do that too many times or you will appear not to be on the ball.

Now that you have thought about yourself in the preparation process (what to wear and how you look, as well as the practicalities of how to get there), it is time to turn your attention to the interview itself and how you can prepare for that.

WHAT DO I KNOW ABOUT THE ORGANISATION?

It is vital that you do your research well and learn about the business of the organisation, or the ideals to which it subscribes, or the purpose of its existence. Where can you find this out?

Chapter 3 on where to find work includes a comprehensive list on researching an organisation for both applying for jobs and the interview (see page 43). You will have been sent some information when you originally applied, if your application was made in response to an advertisement. Read and absorb what they have sent you. If you have made a speculative application that has resulted in an interview, the chances are you will already have done some research. There may be a website, they may have an annual report, press cuttings, information on the Internet, or there may be books, articles in newspapers and magazines that will give you material. Look at the data in the chapter on where to find work to learn about the size of the organisation, the scope of its business, the names of the key players, its mission statement, whether it is motivated solely by profit (are there shareholders to consider?), is it a benevolent organisation? (a charity with aims you subscribe to), and so on.

Armed with this information, you should be able to answer the question of the type, 'What do you know about our organisation?' You could start your response with something like, 'Having looked at your website, I can see that . . .', or, 'I have looked at your recent press coverage and noticed that . . .', or, 'I read the paperwork you sent me and it seems to me that . . .', and relate what you have discovered to what you can bring to the organisation. At the interview, try to match your answers to their needs and not your own.

WHAT ARE THEY TRYING TO FIND OUT?

Essentially, they want to know three things about you:

1. Can you do the job? (They must think you are able otherwise they would not have called you for interview – they want to find out more)
2. Will you fit in? (People usually work with others and they need to know that you are a 'team player' and will be able to work with their existing staff – this does not mean that all the people in the organisation are the same, as good teams work best when they are diverse)
3. What added value will you bring to our organisation? (What is the USP [unique selling point] that would make us take *you* rather than any other candidate?)

Most of the questions you will be asked will relate to one of these three basic needs of the organisation, so when you answer you need to think about your response from their perspective and not your own. Never state anything about yourself that is not true. You may want to expand a little on something that you have really done or a skill that you can demonstrate, but resist any urge to be untruthful in the hope of getting a job, as you will find it much worse to be dismissed when you are found out. And you do not know whom the interviewer may have spoken to about you and what information he/she already has.

Very often the first question is a gentle one to warm you up – as in TV quiz shows where the person in the 'hot seat' gets silly questions just to get them used to being in the limelight. The easiest subject for anyone to talk about should be themselves, as this is the topic about which you are expected to know the most. So 'Tell me about yourself' is often the opener. Women find this very hard to answer. So many members of my groups start with, 'I am a single mother with three children'; 'I have been married for twenty years and have two teenagers'; 'I have been at home with my family for the last ten years' – and so on. I feel that this may not be the best way to start and reflects the sense of self that most women have after being at home for a while.

If you are not sure what the interviewer means, you could ask for clarification: 'Would you like me to tell you about my characteristics or my working background?' Or you could start to say a bit about the kind of person you are and then say, 'I have told you about my main characteristics and personality; was this what you had in mind?' That may lead on to a supplementary question, giving you an opportunity to expand on what you have already said. You could say, 'Would you like me to tell you about what I have been doing in the last few years? Or perhaps something about my work ethic? Are you interested in my family situation?' Or something along those lines. The question may have been deliberately vague to see what you say.

I suggest that you prepare about 200 words about yourself that you can use in response to this approach, or choose parts (a sort of pick and mix) to answer other similar questions. Two hundred words are about 15 lines on this page. Not very much, really. But they will give you confidence that you have prepared something and can be used to answer a variety of personal questions along the lines of:

Tell me about yourself
What are your main characteristics?
What do people like about you?
What sort of things are you good at?
What are your strengths?
How would you describe your personality?
What are your strong points?
Describe yourself in six adjectives.
How would your work colleagues describe you?

The answers to all these questions should be given in relation to the job you are applying for. However good you are at cake baking, if this is not part of the job, it is not relevant at this early stage!

The starting point for this 200-word answer might be the personal profile you have written on your CV. You can expand on this. Finding strong words to mark you out from the other candidates will be time well spent. Take another look at the word power list and see what fits you best. A thesaurus (a book of words grouped together according to their meanings) may also give you ideas for words that are a little different from the usual well-worn phrases. If you have made a skills inventory, which you may have done to prepare your CV, this will help you to prepare the 200 words about yourself. Even if you are not asked this question, the act of preparation itself will help you to be your best at the interview.

If a particular question worries you, try to think of an answer while you are preparing for the interview, as this worry may surface at just the wrong time and contribute to that 'mind-going-blank' moment that we would all like to avoid during an interview. Women with a long career break are often worried about accounting for themselves while they have not been at work and believe that employers do not value time spent at home. Happily, this situation does seem to be changing. Read again the section on the mum's CV (on page 51) to see what skills you may have gained and try to look at them from a business perspective. You have not 'just been a bit involved with the Brownies', you have 'organised and managed the local Brownie pack, including pack holiday for 25 girls, which necessitated considerable tact and diplomacy in dealing with their parents'. Same thing, different spin. I know it is not easy – women so often undervalue what they have done and cannot present it in a context that makes it sound business-like. But this will give you confidence in your abilities, and it does sound impressive.

Some women have expressed a concern about how to deal with an application for a job that is significantly below their abilities. They have made a decision to go for a lower level of work because they are not interested in too much responsibility, or they may not want to take their work home with them (either literally or as a worry), or they may be working just for the money and be happy to get a salary and not worry about status. Women have said that they are concerned that they may not even be called for interview in such a situation, and what should they do?

I wish I had a clear-cut answer. Perhaps you could leave off your Master's degree from your CV; it would be best to focus more on the work to be done in the job and less on your qualifications. You might want to address this concern briefly in your covering letter by saying that you are applying for this job because you really want to do it; you are aware that you may appear over-qualified but will approach it with your customary integrity and high standards. What you have gained from your higher education (the ability to take in information, work things out for yourself) can easily be transferred to this new job. Your additional maturity will ensure that you are reliable, stable, and you are not looking to flit from one job to another.

A skilled employer should not question your decision to apply for any particular post. They should assume that you understand what is required and not make comments like, 'Well, you will be bored in three months and want to leave'.

What other kind of questions are they likely to ask you? No-one can know this exactly, as it will depend on the nature and level of the work you are applying for. If you are hoping to join a high-level team of employment lawyers at a big firm, you would expect the questions to be searching and geared towards demonstrating that you have the intellectual rigour and experience, or potential, to work at that level. If you want to be a school administrator, the questions will be focused at that level and may not be as searching.

But there are generic questions to which any interviewer might want an answer, to get an idea about you as a person, your character, how you deal with pressure (the interview is, after all, very pressured), and how you answer. There may not be a right or wrong answer, just a better or less good way of dealing with it. This can be helped by preparation. Below, I list a few questions that you could think about, write down the answers to, talk to a friend about, record yourself answering – anything to get used to talking in this way and not hesitating or stumbling.

Why do you want this job?
Why do you think you would be successful in this role?
What made you apply for this job?
Describe a time when you felt ineffective. What did you do about
   it and what was the outcome?
What would you say is your greatest weakness?
What is your greatest achievement?

What else do you think we should know about you? (This is likely to be asked near the end of the interview)

Describe a problem you have encountered at work and how you solved it. (If you can't find an example from your work, use one from the rest of your life and relate it to work, especially if it involved dealing tactfully with other people)

By preparing answers to this type of open and rather daunting question, you will be more fluent at the interview and come across with greater confidence. Imagine hearing this type of question and not having the faintest idea how to reply. Preparation is the key to success.

Case Study: Paula

Paula had been out of work for a year. She left a very stressful job at a bank after several colleagues were made redundant and she found herself doing their work as well as her own. The considerable strain this caused forced her to leave. She was worried about explaining this to her prospective employer at the interview when asked, 'Why did you leave your last job?'

At the time that she left her job, she had received a modest inheritance that enabled her to fulfil her life's ambition of climbing a mountain. In the year during which she was out of work, she planned for this climb, joined a group where she did not know anyone at first and participated fully in the expedition to climb her mountain. We discussed this at some length as, for me, that expedition was the ultimate in team-working, where people's lives literally depended on good communication and working well with each other. I asked her if she would have left work at that time, even if she had not been so stressed. She said that she would. I suggested that she focus on the climb as the reason for leaving work and talk about how she grew and developed as a person by facing this challenge (she had never climbed before) as I felt that the interviewer would be struck by her fearlessness.

After the interview, they offered her a job at a higher level than the one she applied for as they were so impressed by her performance there. She turned her greatest fear into a huge advantage and had no need even to think about the negative aspects of leaving her previous job.

You may also be asked some questions to test your areas of vulnerability – try not to perceive them as indications that they are going to reject you. Rather, focus on this chance to reassure the interviewer that, while you may be less strong in one or two areas, you have particular experience/skills/abilities in others. These questions might sound something like:

> Your experience is rather limited. How could you convince us that you can do the job?
>
> You left your last job because you were made redundant – why was this?
>
> You have not got the qualification we were looking for. Why should we take you on?
>
> We were hoping for someone with particular experience in our business. How would you answer our concerns in this area?

They may also just want to see how you react under pressure, especially if the job itself has pressure within it.

WHAT DO YOU WANT TO KNOW ABOUT THE ORGANISATION?

If you already know how long the interview is planned to last, you will have some idea of how many questions they are expecting you to ask, as you will be able to see how much time you have left. Many people want to know about the salary and holiday entitlement, but my feeling is that there is time to talk about that when they really want you. This is the time to show your interest in the organisation and its work, in developing yourself for its benefit and contributing to its success.

Suggested questions for you to ask

> Are there any significant changes in the pipeline that would affect the job I am applying for?
>
> Who will I report to? Is that person here at the interview?
>
> What opportunities are there for training and development?

What are the career prospects here?

How many people are employed here?

What do you feel about time taken out of the workplace? What is your view of a career break?

After the interview it is important to write and thank the people you saw for interviewing you. This advice may sound like your mother telling you what are just good manners but it is becoming increasingly the norm to write after the interview. Suppose that there were two equally good candidates and one had written a thank-you letter and the other had not – which do you think would get the job? The letter does not need to be too long or too gushing, just a simple thank you for their time. If you really liked the organisation you could add something along the lines of, 'Having had the opportunity to meet you and see the organisation, it has reinforced my interest in working with you and I hope that I shall have the opportunity to do so.'

What if you decide that, whatever happens, you would not take a job there? I think it would be courteous to say so in your letter, but *only* if you are absolutely sure. You can always reject an offer after it is made but you will not get another chance if you write to say no thanks, before it comes.

But if you are sure, or if something happens in between that changes your situation (you win the Lottery, your partner gets transferred to New York, your mother becomes ill, your child needs an operation – the possibilities are endless), then it would be appropriate to write. After the initial thank you, you could say, 'Since meeting you, my circumstances have changed and I have now decided not to pursue my application with your organisation. I hope you will find the best candidate for this post' – or wording along similar lines. They will appreciate the fact that they will not be wasting time on your application.

The thank-you letter is even more necessary when you have met someone as a result of a speculative letter, as they have made special time for you. This should be along similar lines but include some comment about the fact that you appreciate their time as they are very busy, not actively recruiting at the moment, fitted you in, etc. If you have been put in contact by a third party (friend, colleague, etc.), it would also be polite to write to thank them for making the introduction and to keep them informed of your progress.

Some of the women I have worked with have been uncomfortable about sending a thank-you letter after an interview as they feel that it makes them look desperate for a job, as though this is their only chance. Although I do not agree, I can see how someone who is desperate might not want to reveal that they are, and that this letter might suggest it.

If you are thinking this, consider whether someone who is in work would only ever apply for one job – I do not think so. The chances of applying for one job and getting it after interview are remote – it does happen, but usually the process takes a little longer and requires persistence. With this in mind, the employer will also know that you may well be applying for more than one job and will therefore be unlikely to think that he/she is your only chance and that you are desperate. Try and substitute 'keen and enthusiastic' for 'desperate' and you may have a different spin on the situation. The trick is to make the employer feel that you really want to work in his/her organisation, you care about improving it and will be a valuable addition to the team. This comes with the preparation we have discussed.

I have been asked by women about how to negotiate a salary. While there are several good books devoted entirely to this subject, I think you might get some valuable information from Richard Bolles' book, *What Color is Your Parachute?* which includes a section on how to negotiate your salary at the upper end of what the employer is offering. (See reading list for details.) In many cases there will be no negotiation – the salary is fixed and you may have been told what it is when you applied. But sometimes there is room to persuade an employer that you will be good value for money and the salary is sometimes expressed in the advertisement as 'AAE' – according to age and experience. (See page 244 for other examples of these useful-to-know abbreviations.) By asking around to find out what is the going rate for the type of work you want to do, you should be able to gain an idea of what you are worth.

My final word to you on the subject of interviews is to remember the five 'P's: **P**roper **P**reparation **P**revents **P**oor **P**erformance.

'Failing to prepare is preparing to fail.'

8

Work-life balance and coping strategies

'If you knew Time as well as I do, you wouldn't talk about wasting it. I daresay you never even spoke to Time. Now if you only kept on good terms with him, he'd do anything you like with the clock.' – the Mad Hatter, Alice's Adventures in Wonderland

Having looked at your skills, prepared a CV with which you are happy, applied for jobs, and been successful at interview, the challenge is now to make it all work and fit your new job or career into your existing lifestyle. You don't want to find that after three months at work you are on your knees as you try to be the best at everything and feel that you are doing nothing properly.

It is all about getting the balance in your life to be the best it can be at any given moment. I do not believe that perfection exists in this area – there are too many variables and things are changing all the time. Just when you think that it is all hanging together nicely, something comes along, perhaps a total bolt from the blue, perhaps something you have already seen or felt looming on the horizon, which tips the balance one way or another and you have to start reassessing your situation.

What I hope to do in this chapter is to look at your life as a whole, with all its constituent parts, and see how you have divided up your time between areas and how you can prioritise them. This will enable you to optimise the time you spend on each and feel that you are in control of your life and it is not running away with you.

Looking at work-life balance applies to everyone, but is especially relevant for a woman returner as the demands on your time from the period when you were not working are less likely to have disappeared. The roles you have been playing – wife, mother, daughter, sister, volunteer, etc. – may still be there, as well as the new one of career woman or employee. The trick is to fit it all in so that you feel the effort is worthwhile. It will not be easy and I cannot promise you a seamless transition from one state to another. If you have succeeded in doing this, fantastic – I envy you, and you are likely to be in a minority. Most of us lurch from one day to the next, grateful that we have done most of what we wanted to do, and fall into bed, to wake the next day with still more to do. Superwoman, that mythical female who is often discussed in newspaper articles, probably does not exist. By writing about some women who seem to have found the answer to 'having it all', journalists make those of us who are struggling in an ordinary way feel as though we are failing if we are not perfect mummies, ideal daughters, seductive wives and thoroughly successful career women. We need to understand that we can only do what we can and if we are able to examine our lives and decide what is really important for us, then we can look ourselves in the mirror each night and say, 'I am doing my best'.

I see everyone's life as a pie or a cake – the whole thing can be divided into slices of different sizes. Each slice represents a different part of your life, some larger and some smaller, depending on how much attention you are devoting to each part at any given time. And this will be constantly changing according to circumstances, some within and some outside your control. But the whole remains a constant size – whatever you do, the day has only 24 hours and there are only seven days in the week (my request from a fairy godmother would be for an extra day in the week which no-one else has, to do all the boring but essential things that I keep postponing!).

It is also about managing your time well and getting the most out of your efforts. To analyse how you are spending your time, you could make a grid of your day, as below, and fill it in for one week (yes, I know it takes time to do this but it will be worth it) to see how you are spending your time, on what, and what roles you are playing (e.g. cook, chauffeur, negotiator, laundry maid, peace-maker, etc.). This will also help you with your skills inventory if you are still working on that.

Time	Tasks done	Skills used
6.00am 7.00am 8.00am And so on, until 10.00pm 11.00pm		

WHAT ARE THE ELEMENTS THAT MAKE UP YOUR LIFE?

Here are a few suggestions for what some slices of your 'cake' might be concerned with (there will be others that I have not thought of):

- Your health/sports life
- Your financial life
- Your work or career
- Your intimate relationships
- Your family/extended family
- Your social life and friends
- Your community/voluntary work
- Your spiritual/religious life
- Your pets
- Your domestic responsibilities

Let us take a moment to look at these individually so that you can consider what size slice each occupies at the moment and how much you can realistically devote to them when you are returning to work.

The most important element in your life is your **health**. Without good health you cannot function at your best and many of the people you support or help will also suffer if you are not well, or unable to function properly. Most women are at the centre of their family's life as well as their own. Generally speaking, if your elderly mother is ill or needs help, you are the person she will call; if your children are ill or have an accident, you will be there for them; if there is a crisis in the family, you will be the one who needs to sort it out. This is not to denigrate the support and help of brothers, husbands, fathers or partners, but from the hundreds of women with whom I have worked,

I have gleaned the fact that this is just how it is. I am very happy to be the lynchpin in my own family, it makes me feel good to be needed, but I also know that I need to be in tip-top condition to be able to cope with it all, and that is not always the case.

If you have a medical problem causing you intermittent trouble, or some other issue of health that needs attending to, do try to deal with it before you return to work, especially if you are selling yourself in your CV as utterly reliable and committed. It may be hard for you to be that person if every month you are in bed for two days, or suffer from migraines so badly that you are unable to work when you get one. I know that this is easier said than done, but if any health issues apply to you, please consider how you can deal with them so that they are not a problem in terms of your reliability at work.

Over the years I have found that some sort of regular exercise is a great way to maintain better health. I have noticed that women returning to work often catch coughs and colds, especially if they are travelling to work on public transport. My theory is that you are immune to the bugs and infections floating around in your familiar environment, but when you meet all these new ones on the train or bus you succumb. I have no hard scientific evidence to back this up, but dozens of women have told me that this has been the case for them. Perhaps now is the time to start taking extra care of yourself with the food you eat, the exercise you take and any vitamins you feel you might need as a boost to your ability to withstand common infections.

Perhaps you enjoy swimming, walking, tennis, netball – the list is endless, but there is much more to be gained from these activities than just physical fitness. I also book 'gym' into my diary and do not cancel unless there is an emergency. I feel that it is important to look after my well-being as so many other people depend on me. I hope you will be able to find some time for yourself in whatever way you can.

We all need **money** to live and it is often the main reason why women return to work – just to pay the bills. Even if you are returning for other reasons – we have spent quite some time on those in chapter 2 – making ends meet financially is vital for us all. Look carefully at the true cost of returning to work – travel, parking, childcare, clothes, etc., and see whether it is all worth it. You may find that you are working at first just to cover your childcare costs, which are usually very high, unless you have a mother around to help you regularly, but you may consider it an investment in your future career. As your children get older, those expenses may diminish, but it is still a good use of your time to see how much you need to earn to make it all worth it. The hassle of working, organising the children, making arrangements for your elderly parents, having someone to look after your pets – is it all worth it for an extra £30 a week? (And do not forget the taxman in all of this! See Appendix 3 providing basic financial information at the end of the book for additional help.)

Some people have independent means, not connected with their work. If you are one of those, then see how much time you are spending on managing your investments. Can you take that time out to return to work, and will someone else manage your finances to the same standard?

Work or career do not currently feature in your life if you are reading this book with the intention of returning. But how much time will it take up when you are successful in getting back to work, and how much time do you want it to take up? If you are only available to work between 2 and 3pm on Wednesday afternoons, given your present work-life balance, you do need to reassess how you are spending your time. Do you know how many hours you want to work and does this take into account travelling time? As well as the time factor, there is the mental energy – your work may cause you to worry about certain elements within the job; your level of responsibility may mean that you are never 'off duty' and get frequent calls at home; you may be running your own business and be driving yourself harder than any employee – there are many other aspects to consider but these are just to get you thinking about the reality of working and fitting it in to the pattern of your work-life balance.

If you are **married or in a relationship**, you will need to include time with your husband or partner as one of the slices of your cake – it is easy to forget that even long-standing couples need to spend time together to ensure that they do not grow stale or, even worse, apart. One couple I know book out every Wednesday evening for a 'date' and ensure that they spend some quality time together. In a life that is very full or hectic, it is very important that we do not neglect those who are closest to us.

Perhaps you spend time with your grandmother every week, perhaps your parents have a regular slot in your life, perhaps your children are totally dependent on you for their social life because you are a lone parent, or your other half is away a great deal, or you live in a rather isolated area. For whatever reason, your **extended family** may have a significant claim on your time. Think carefully if you do want to say to your grandmother that you will no longer have time to take her out or visit her, once you start working. That may be a very precious relationship, and, to state the obvious, may not always be there for you to enjoy either. You may feel guilty at not being able to spend so much time with your family. This is something you need to work out in your own mind before you return to work and discover that it is three months since you last saw your nearest and dearest.

And what about your **friends and your social life**? Perhaps you have women friends you see regularly but will not be able to meet once you are back at work? Perhaps they too are thinking about returning and won't be available for you anyway, but it is worth considering. You may enjoy entertaining but could find that, after returning to work, there is no time for shopping and cooking when you have friends over, as you are so tired from just managing your home and the job. I am not saying it will be like this, but do think about how you spend your time and where changes are likely to occur. When I returned to work, I found meeting old friends much more difficult but we keep in touch by email. Our pattern of socialising has changed and we tend to go out more so that none of us is cooking, or we each bring something and just 'muck in', as we are all too busy for what I call 'posh entertaining'.

Most women I have worked with do some sort of **voluntary work** outside the home but within their own communities – either for their local church or other religious group, or the Guides or Scouts, or maybe helping at school with literacy or being on a charity committee. If you are returning to paid work, you may find that you just do not have time for these very valuable and worthwhile contributions to the community, which you might consider a shame. You might prefer to think about work that still allows you to give some time and effort to others if you are getting something out of it yourself. It may be that you will think that you have given enough time to others and can extricate yourself comfortably from your commitments. You may need to tell the organisation for which you volunteer that you are thinking about returning to work, as they may be relying on you and need some notice to replace you. Alternatively, they may offer you a paid job in order to keep your talent and experience – it has happened to more than one of my clients.

Case Study: Joanna

Joanna had given up work to be at home with her three children. She had previously worked in marketing with a background in information science and was not sure what she could do as a returner that would fit in with her family. Her main priority was to be able to manage the children's day and she wanted to fit in a job around that, preferably part-time. While she was researching what to do, she accepted a position for one day a week doing voluntary work at one of her local National Trust sites, to gain some experience. Arriving on her first day, she learned that one member of staff, the 'group and educational visits organiser', was leaving immediately. The next day, feeling, she admits, 'rather pushy', she rang the relevant person to ask whether she might fill that post temporarily while they looked for a replacement, and on a part-time basis. They agreed to take her for two days a week, and although the pay is not good, she enjoys it greatly. The hands-on aspect of the job is stimulating, seeing things happen immediately, and crucial, she says, is 'being able to leave it all behind when I go home'. Before our session she would not have had the impetus to ask about paid work in that voluntary organisation; she hopes that her experience of turning voluntary work into paid work after one day might be useful for other women. She was just in the right place at the right time.

Not everyone has a **religious or spiritual** side, but if you do it may be a fairly large slice of the cake that is your life. For some people, this involves regular visits to their place of worship, and significant effort to maintain a home and atmosphere within it that is in keeping with their religious values. If this applies to you, think about how much time you are spending each day or week on this part of your life, and ask whether there are likely to be any problems with managing this and returning to work? Are there days of the week, or times of the year when you are less likely to be available to work? Some people plan their lives around religious demands and you may need to see what is really important to you and how much your new job or career will impact on this aspect.

I have also included **pets** in this list as many people spend quite some time looking after their animals. I know some women who have planned their working lives so that they are able to continue walking the dog in their lunch-hour, or otherwise look after their pets.

Domestic responsibilities take up a significant slice of most women's lives and one where there is often less choice about involvement. Shopping for food, preparing and clearing it up, washing and ironing, keeping your home clean and tidy – these tasks usually fall to women and seem endless. (Well, they are!) Delegating where possible will help reduce the size of this piece of your cake, especially as there is not huge joy in some of the tasks, compared to other elements of your life. Some useful tips have included pinning socks together after wearing and before washing to save time on sorting and to prevent wearing mis-matched pairs; cooking twice the amount of food and freezing half for another day when time is short; learning to ignore mess which is not directly in your line of vision; teaching even quite young children to clear up after themselves; making a chart of domestic responsibilities so that everyone takes a turn at helping. Even a small improvement can make a huge difference to one's mental state on facing these mundane and repetitive tasks.

These are only suggestions about areas to think about and all will not apply to you. They provide starting points and can be useful in seeing where you are expending your energies and where you might be able to free up some time. Where are you going to fit a job in your already full life, if that is the case? Maybe you are bored at home. You have certainly been doing more at home than you thought you were.

Many women, as well as trying to juggle their working and home lives, are at the centre of other people's lives, especially their children's, or sometimes their parents'. If you are not well, not only does your life suffer but theirs does too. Please allow your children to approach the washing machine, or teach your other half to use it as well, so even if you are ill the clothes still get washed!

A word here about letting go – which some women find very difficult. We do see certain tasks as 'our territory' or want our home to look a particular way. I have spoken to many groups about this very sensitive subject. If you want others to help you, to shift the balance within your home and share the tasks out more evenly, you have to accept the manner in which they are done and loosen your control in this area. This is not easy to do, and many women want the kitchen to be as they like it, and their home to reflect the standard which they set. If this is you, then you must either do it yourself – and stop complaining, either out loud or inwardly – or you may delegate it in some way and accept that, while it may not be done to your own standards or in your own way, you are not doing it and it frees up time for you to do something else. You cannot do it all – it is not possible.

To help you consider what is really important for you to do yourself, to keep hold of, and what you can comfortably delegate, I have produced a very simple grid, which you can copy and relate to your own situation. Ideally, if you had time, you could make one for each area of your life and apply these questions to it.

What must I keep hold of?	What can I delegate?
What can I put on the back burner?	**What can I jettison completely?**

Case Study: Deirdre

Deirdre had been at home looking after her large family, for whom she provided a home-cooked meal every night. Eating together was a very important part of their family life and even after she returned to work, by which time her children were all teenagers, she was still maintaining the same high standards.

One evening, when she returned late from work, she found her husband and four children spread-eagled in front of the television, asking her 'What's for supper?' as she walked into the house. She exploded with the frustration of exhaustion and the realisation that everyone was still expecting her to do all the domestic things she had been doing as well as her new job. She needed to take action. She took her husband out for a meal and told him that she was on her knees, both physically and mentally. He was upset that he had not noticed the situation and wanted to know what he could do to help. She had tried to be 'Superwoman' and do everything herself and was only now realising that it was not possible.

Deirdre suggested that he take control of the evening meal one night a week, with the assistance of the children, and she would have nothing to do with that meal except to eat it. It could be supper at home, a take-away, a meal out, or just beans on toast week in and week out, but there was an understanding that she would also not comment at all, even if the kitchen were in a mess and the air blue with strong language. This one relatively small change made a huge difference to her work-life balance, as is so often the case. Even a little change can have a large impact.

When we delegate a task to someone else, whether at home or in a work environment, we need to think how we feel about losing control of that particular task – we may feel that it is 'our territory' or we may not think that another person can do it as well as we would, or to our high standard.

If we enjoy that task, or elements within it, it may be difficult to hand it over and sacrifice something that gives us pleasure or personal satisfaction. Perhaps you would prefer to delegate the tasks that you do not particularly enjoy – ironing comes to mind for me, but there are many tasks which have to be done but do not need to be done by you personally.

We tend to believe that we are invincible and can do everything – delegating means there is some (reluctant) acceptance that we cannot cope, and some women find this very hard to come to terms with. They want to show that they are 'Superwoman' and can take on anything and not collapse. But we do not need to be so keen to prove ourselves – and we do not set a good role model for our children when we take this attitude. Asking for help is not a sign of weakness or inability to cope, and may be greeted by a keen response from your family and friends if you ask in a genuine way. You have to decide what it is you are not prepared to delegate, i.e. what you *must* keep hold of, for whatever reason.

Perhaps you want to be the one who collects your child at the school gate – in that case you need to organise work so that you are there and not in a meeting in the centre of town at 3.30. Maybe you like to make your own food, bread, cakes, and so on. This takes a huge amount of time and organisation but if it is important to you, then you will make time for it, and plan your working life accordingly. Perhaps you want to have 20 minutes' relaxation every day to be able to cope with all that you have to do, and you need to establish your ground rules so that you can do this without being disturbed. Look at the elements within your life, at all the parts of it listed at the beginning of this chapter and see what your priorities are – then insert them into the grid and see what you must do yourself and what you can delegate. Many women find that domestic duties – cleaning, ironing, etc. – fit into this category and they are happy to pay someone else to do them, especially when they have a little more money when they are working. It may be cost-effective to do so.

Some things may be in your life at the moment but need to be put on the back-burner until you are settled in your new job and everything seems to slot into place. I use the analogy of an aeroplane taking off for this stage. Take-off uses the most energy – once the plane is up in the air it cruises along smoothly and easily. Returning to work is a bit like that – it requires a lot of your energy at the start with organisation and adaptation to the new balance of your life. Once things settle down it is much easier just to cruise along, and then perhaps put back into your life those activities that had to take a back seat. Perhaps you are doing a course, perhaps you visit someone, perhaps you are learning a new skill and need to stop temporarily until the balance of your life changes again, as it surely will.

The last quarter of the grid allows you to see what you can jettison completely to make room for other things. This can be very liberating but may need to be done with tact and diplomacy if it involves other people.

The whole point about work-life balance is that it is constantly changing and we need to adapt to those changes. Life is rarely static and if you are able to develop a strategy for yourself you will be able to deal with the changes and not feel that it is all crashing down around you. The image of scales, tipping the balance when something else happens, works very well for me. At different times in your life the balance will change in ways you can probably predict:

- When your children are young, they need more of your hands-on time (they do still need you when they are older, but in a different way)
- When your job is new, or when your business is new if you are self-employed, you may have to put in more time to establish yourself either with an employer or within your industry or field of work
- Should your marriage be threatened, you will need to devote more time to your relationship, and should divorce be what happens next, that will also take up your time until the issues are resolved
- If your parents are ill, you may be the one who must care for them, do their shopping, take them to hospital appointments and so on, or at the very least make arrangements for someone else to do these tasks
- If you are not well yourself, you will need to take time to recover your health, or adapt to your new status, depending on what the issues are
- You may become a grandmother and want to include time in your week to see your grandchild as well as working

These are only a few examples of the kind of situations that can change the balance of our lives.

Here I would like to reproduce a little story to illustrate how to prioritise. It goes like this:

I attended a seminar once where the instructor was lecturing on time. At one point he said, 'OK, it's time for a quiz.' He reached under the table and pulled out a wide-mouth gallon jar. He set it on the table next to a platter with some fist-sized rocks on it. 'How many of these rocks do you think we can get in the jar?' he asked. After we made our guess, he said, 'OK, let's find out.' He set one rock in the jar . . . then another . . . then another. I don't remember how many he got in, but he got the jar full. Then he asked, 'Is that jar full?' Everybody looked at the rocks and said, 'Yes.' Then he said, 'Ahhh.' He reached under the table and pulled out a bucket of gravel. Then he dumped some gravel in and shook the jar and the gravel went in all the little spaces left by the big rocks. Then he grinned and said once more, 'Is the jar full?' By this time we were on to him. 'Probably not,' we said. 'Good!' he replied. And he reached under the table and brought out a bucket of sand. He started dumping the sand in and it went in all the little spaces left by the rocks and the gravel. Once more he looked at us and said, 'Is the jar full?' 'No!' we all roared. He said, 'Good!' and he grabbed a pitcher of water and began to pour it in. He got something like a quart of water in that jar. Then he said, 'Well, what's the point?' Somebody said, 'Well, there are gaps, and if you really work at it, you can always fit more into your life.'

'No,' he said. 'That's not the point. The point is this: if you hadn't put these big rocks in first, would you ever have gotten any of them in?'

(Excerpt from Steven Covey, Roger and Rebecca Merrill, First Things First, *1994, © Franklin Covey Co., used with permission. All rights reserved.)*

For me, the rocks represent the really important things in your life and the story shows that you need to put those in first. The water represents the least important elements in your life. If you filled the jar with water first, you would never get any of the other things in at all. You need to decide what the rocks in your life are – they will be different for everyone – and then ensure that you are putting them first, prioritising them in your life. The rest will fit in, occupying the spaces between the rocks. By looking at your life and seeing what really is important to you, you may be able to find a balance that works well, that reduces the stress you feel, and increases your belief that you are doing what matters.

I feel that this is something to strive towards, rather than actually hope to achieve – like the Chinese proverb, 'It is better to travel hopefully than to arrive'. I know very few people who feel that the balance of their life is perfect but we are all trying to get there, and in doing so, we are managing as best we can.

WHAT HAPPENS WHEN YOU ARE NOT COPING WELL?

> *'Every now and then go away, have a little relaxation, for when you come back to your work, your judgement will be surer, since to remain constantly at work will cause you to lose your power of judgement.'* – Leonardo da Vinci

While the management of stress is a totally separate subject covered in many excellent books, here are a few suggestions for trying to defuse a stressful situation when your life feels as though it is all getting too much. The ideal would be not to get in that state in the first place, but we are all human and we do get swamped sometimes. Try to drink water every day. We need it to function well and if you can increase your daily intake to about 2 litres (eight glasses is suggested) you will feel the benefit. I am told that it is better to sip it gradually than gulp it down a glass at a time as it tends to be absorbed better in small doses.

Active relaxation

Try to take some time for yourself, with a meditation tape or just going for a gentle walk, away from it all, to give yourself some thinking time. Even 20 minutes a day can make a difference but you may feel that the only way to manage this is to get out of your home, as people always seem to find you when you are trying to grab a few moments 'me-time'. If you are not there, they can't. Clearly, this is harder to do with small children around, but perhaps you can manage some time in the evening if you are able to get someone to stay with them for a short time.

Exercise or sport

As mentioned already, exercise is a great stress-buster and if you are able to get some (swimming, running, brisk walking) you might feel noticeably more able to cope afterwards. This will help to reduce your stress levels, especially if you can do it regularly.

Take a holiday/weekend away

A complete break from your normal environment with a holiday or even weekend away can renew you and make you feel able to cope. This is not always practical (or affordable) but can do wonders if you can manage it.

Pamper yourself

In the absence of a holiday away, try to pamper yourself, undisturbed at home, if you can. Have a sweet-smelling bath, with little candles and low lighting, give yourself a pedicure, do your nails, read a girlie magazine – anything that takes you away both physically and mentally from your stressed situation even for a few hours. You will feel better able to cope.

Chat with a good friend

If you have a close friend you can talk to, then now is the time to let off steam and tell her how you are feeling. You will probably be there for her when she is feeling the same, and having someone to listen to your troubles can be very liberating. Just talking about them can put them into perspective and a solution often comes to you at the same time.

Listen to or play music

If you are musical, you may already use music as relaxation, either by playing or listening to your favourites. Immersing yourself in classical music really can make all the cares of the day disappear. But you may prefer something else – or, indeed, you may play the piano, or guitar, or any other instrument that allows you to be carried away by the music for a short while.

Walking the dog

A recent newspaper article reported that people with pets had lower levels of stress than those without. It may be all the walking that has a beneficial effect, or the stroking that keeps the stress levels low, but your pet might be the key to a healthier lifestyle.

Retail therapy

Many women find shopping relaxing and enjoy it greatly, cheering themselves up by buying something, even if it is a lipstick or some other little item. Retail therapy does not have to involve spending large amounts of money – but the results can be really worth it!

So what do you need to make it all balance?

The quote below gives an excellent perspective on what is important in life. In the next chapter you will find a suggested list for pulling all the strands together and making a successful transition.

> *'Imagine life as a game in which you are juggling some five balls in the air. You name them: work, family, health, friends and spirit, and you're keeping all of these in the air. You will soon understand that work is a rubber ball. If you drop it, it will bounce back. But the other four balls – family, health, friends and spirit – are made of glass. If you drop one of these, they will be irrevocably scuffed, marked, nicked, damaged, or even shattered. They will never be the same.*
>
> *You must understand that and strive for balance in your life.' – Brian Dyson, CEO, Coca Cola Enterprises*

9

Final countdown and confidence-building

'Be confident. Even if you are not, pretend to be. No-one can tell the difference.' – Life's Little Instruction Book

I hope that by the time you have reached this point you will have a strong idea of what you are good at, an understanding of why you want to return to work, and a strategy for stretching your life to include a return to the workplace.

What are my final words to you to help you make that move as successfully as possible? Well, I have a checklist of things that I think you probably need to make a smooth transition from where you are now to where you want to be. If you have decided that the time is not right, or that it is too much hassle for not enough money, or that you really want to be at home now, that is great. Finding out what you do *not* want to do is as important as finding out what you *do* want to do. And taking the time to read this book may have given you ways of dealing with your response to the 'what do you do' question, or the well-meaning friends who are trying to plan your life by suggesting that you are 'ready to return to work now'. You can look them in the eye and, with total confidence, say that you have thought about returning to work but for the moment have decided that you are happy to be at home. You might rethink later on but you are quite happy with your decision at the moment. And *believe it!*

If you have decided that, despite all the obstacles I have mentioned, and the challenge required of you to make it work, not to mention the effort you need to prepare your applications, you are still keen to return, here are my thoughts for you at this exciting time in your life.

WHAT DO YOU NEED TO MAKE IT ALL WORK?

1) Recognition of your own skills

Without knowing what you are good at, what your main character strengths are and what you consider your main achievements, you cannot begin to sell yourself as a prospective candidate to an employer, or even to set up your own business, if that is what you want to do. Self-analysis is crucial to the process.

2) A CV that does you justice

Having taken time to assess yourself, you need to put the results down on paper and ensure that your CV properly reflects what you have done and your potential to an employer. Even if you are required to complete an application form, the preparation of the CV can be used to fill in the sections of the form. It will not be wasted effort.

3) More qualifications possibly?

After reading this book, and researching possible careers, you may have reached the conclusion that you need more qualifications. Perhaps you want to get that degree you have always thought about, perhaps you are thinking about doing garden design and would like a qualification in that; maybe you want to be a classroom or learning support assistant and have found out about a course at your local college. Or you would like to work towards a Master's degree and now is the right time for you. I hope that you will know how to find the relevant information and not be afraid to take on the new challenge of studying. You will also be setting your children an excellent example by showing them that education and further study are to be valued at any stage of life. And any effort you may need to make to get this further qualification will be temporary and a stepping stone to re-entering the employment market at a higher level.

4) Improve your IT (Information Technology) skills

Whatever work you plan to do, it is highly likely that you will need to know how to use a computer – at the very least you should be able to write a letter, send emails, search the Internet and use a basic spreadsheet. There are many courses now (further information in the directory at the end of this book) and the ECDL (European Computer Driving Licence) is universally recognised. It is called a driving licence as it indicates a basic standard level of computer literacy, in the same way that a driving licence indicates basic competencies behind the wheel.

5) A mentor/adviser/counsellor

Having someone to talk to and bounce ideas off is very valuable. Many organisations are introducing mentoring schemes where more experienced employees are paired with less experienced ones, in a sort of 'buddying' system. Questions can be asked in a safe environment and both parties can feel comfortable sharing ideas. A friend who will do this for you can provide an outlet that you value greatly, and this can also be reciprocal – you can do it for her as well. An outsider can often see more clearly than someone very close to a situation. You may also use someone in a professional (i.e. paid) capacity for this role. Either way, it is better if it is someone with whom you do not have an emotional involvement, so there is some level of detachment.

6) A supportive husband/partner/family

Feeling that those at home are totally supportive of what you are trying to do can make a significant impact on the success of returning to work. It is important that you share with your partner and the rest of your immediate family how you feel about your situation, why you want to return to work and what the implications are for everyone in the household. It may be at the most basic level of sharing out household duties (or learning to shut your eyes if they are not done), or at the emotional level of understanding that in the short term you may need to give your attention to establishing yourself in your new job. It may also be moral support when things do not go well – a feeling that you can share your disappointments with those who want you to succeed as much as you do. If your mother is going to keep saying to you, 'But you never have any time for me lately', that will not help you. And family members complaining that the laundry service has deteriorated need to understand that they may need to take responsibility for their own washing, if they are old enough. Perhaps a meal out with all your nearest and dearest to explain to them the possible changes will help them to be more supportive of your new life.

7) A sympathetic employer

Research that I have carried out informally with my groups of women returners indicates that what they most want from employers are flexibility and an understanding of their position. Employers who make it easy for women to deal with their (hopefully infrequent) family crises will be rewarded by loyalty, commitment and employees they can trust to get the job done. If your employer offers you childcare, if he or she has taken the trouble to provide a crèche, for example, it can make you feel that it's OK to be a parent and an employee, and that the employer values what parents bring to the workplace. Even if you work for yourself, and many women are looking at self-employment when they think about re-entering the world of work, do not be harder on yourself than you would be on an employee.

8) Lots of energy

Fitting everything in may require you to have great reserves of stamina. If you are naturally someone with great reserves of energy, it will be easier for you to juggle all your different roles when trying to manage home, job and all the other elements in your life. It will be harder for you if you come home from work totally exhausted, collapse in a chair, and never want to get up again. When I was working at the University of Westminster, I used to start to prepare the evening meal with my coat still on, to make the best use of the time, and was often ironing shirts at 11.00 at night. You need stamina to do this, as you will probably need to get up earlier than you did before you were working, just to fit it all in.

9) The ability to compartmentalise your life

Being able to put domestic worries out of your mind while at work, and *vice versa*, is vital. Some women find this extremely difficult but it is essential that when you are working you are giving your mind entirely to the work in hand.

10) Effective means of releasing stress

Feeling stressed is inevitable so you will need to learn how to cope with it. The previous chapter on work-life balance makes some suggestions and it is important to build in time for yourself.

11) Good organisation

Being well-organised is certainly very important to the success of the return-to-work process. You need to know where you are to be at what time, and where your children or other dependents need to be as well. If you need to be at work at 9am and the journey takes you an hour, what arrangements must you make for that to happen? (A report published in July 2003 showed that in the UK our journey to and from work takes longer than any other EU country.) If you have to have sports kit ready for school, reports written to meet deadlines at work, birthday parties organised for children, visits to elderly relatives, you need an efficient system – diary, personal organiser, lists, mind-maps – whatever you are comfortable with. A family diary at home where all the children write in their arrangements – 'If it isn't in the diary, it doesn't happen' – is a good idea. So communicating effectively within the household is vital to being well-organised. Sharing out the domestic duties, either formally with some sort of chart or rota, or informally each day, will contribute greatly. Most women have too much to do and not enough time – if you can prioritise what you must do yourself and what you can delegate each day, that will help. As my mother always says, 'Organisation is the key to success'.

12) Determination

If you are really sure that this is what you want to do, try not to let disappointments along the way sway you from your purpose. Looking for a job means setting yourself up for the possibility of *not* getting one, of exposing yourself to rejection. Without determination you may find that you give up too soon, when success could be waiting for you round the next corner. I know this is not easy, as you need to have the confidence that you will succeed and confidence is a very fragile thing, easily dented. As Wayne Dyer said, **'It's never crowded along the extra mile.'** So success is there for those who do not give up easily and you need determination to see it through.

13) No guilt (if possible!)

I think women are programmed to feel guilty when they are doing things for themselves. I have more press cuttings about the guilt that working mothers feel than on most other topics. Is the fact that we are at work the reason why our children are not achieving well at school? Has my husband found another woman because I have been concentrating on my career? Is it my fault that my mother fell over because I was not there for her? The guilt-ridden questions are endless. I think that you need to trust yourself that you are doing the best you can, given the information you have at the moment. If you are doing your best, that is all you can ask of yourself. Perfection does not exist – and who is to say that working mothers are responsible for the ills that befall society today? A woman who is working at whatever fulfils and satisfies her is likely to be a better mother, wife, partner or daughter just because she feels that she is achieving her potential in whatever field. Feeling frustrated at home, and taking it out on all those around you, is not a recipe for successful relationships. So don't feel guilty.

14) Reliable childcare

I know that I have mentioned this before, but good childcare is crucial, especially for women with young children. If possible, try to get childcare in place before you start looking for a job, as it will make it easier for you to approach an interview without that nagging doubt at the back of your mind – what am I going to do with the baby/children? On page 12 I look at all the options I can think of, and there may be more as well. If you cannot return to work without proper childcare, and you do not have it, you have no choice and must stay at home until the situation changes and the balance of your life shifts again. It is harsh, but it is not unusual that women have to make childcare arrangements, putting their own careers or aspirations on hold while their children are young. But having spent a great deal of time at home with my children, it was, more in hindsight than at the time, really important to me to be there. If this turns out to be your situation, make the best of it until your childcare needs change – even if you are returning for financial reasons, you may find that you are spending so much on childcare that it is really not worth it. Perhaps you can find some work from home that will mean you will not incur childcare expenses.

15) To be taken seriously

If, in talking about returning to work, you are seen to be 'playing' at it or approaching the process with less integrity than you should, you will not be taken seriously, and this will dent your confidence even further. Do think it through before you 'go public' – you may find people only too willing to help you and if you have rushed into telling them, you might be in the embarrassing position of not being able to follow through. If you have done your homework properly and have realistic aims and goals for your present situation, then you should be taken seriously as someone who has worked things out. Even if you are capable of running a department in a large law firm, if you have not sorted your domestic arrangements you will not be able to do it and will lose credibility.

16) Belief in yourself

This is closely linked with confidence – the one thing that everyone mentions to me when they talk about returning to work, and who they were before. 'I have lost my confidence' they all say. But you can find it again – it is only hiding, not lost forever.

Case Study: Hilary
Hilary had been out of paid work for more than 15 years, staying at home to bring up her children in a traditional family environment. She had previously worked in the fashion industry but had suffered a huge loss of confidence while being out of the workplace. Before she came on the returners' course, she did not know where to start the return-to-work journey and had lost her sense of identity as well as her confidence. After a 12-week course, taking a serious look at her own abilities and skills, and talking to the other participants, she felt that she did have something to offer, and left the course with a strong belief in herself. She wrote, 'I feel that due to my confidence building, my aspirations may be higher than I would have originally thought. Thank you for setting me on the path to finding myself again.'

Believing that you can do something, in whatever field, is critical to success. 'Whether you think you can, or whether you think you can't, you are probably right.' Remember that.

I reprint below some wise words on confidence building from Andrew Risner's book, *Empowerment at Work* (reprinted with his permission).

> *Many women experience mixed feelings about what the future holds for them with regard to getting back to work*

and it would be unnatural not to feel a little apprehensive. It helps to know you are not alone and that most people have at some time felt like that. Once you realise that these feelings are perfectly normal you can then work on building your self-confidence.

If you are self-confident you:

- *Have positive yet realistic views of yourself*
- *Have a general sense of control in your life*
- *Believe that, within reason, you will be able to do what you set out to achieve*
- *Are willing to risk the disapproval of others because you generally trust your own abilities*
- *Tend to accept yourself as you are without feeling that you have to conform in order to be accepted*

If you are not self-confident, you:

- *Depend excessively on the approval of others in order to feel good about yourself*
- *Avoid taking risks in case you fail*
- *Do not expect to be successful*
- *Often put yourself down and tend to discount or ignore any compliments you may receive*

Strategies for developing confidence:

- *Don't expect too much from yourself. Being self-confident does not mean you will be able to do everything*
- *Set yourself realistic targets and you will be more likely to meet them. Even when some of these targets are not met, continue to be positive and to accept yourself*
- *Emphasise your strengths*
- *Give yourself credit for everything you try. Be encouraged by the fact that you have tried something rather than by the end product*

- *Take risks. Treat each new experience as an opportunity to learn rather than an occasion to win or lose. By doing this you open up new possibilities and are more likely to accept yourself. Not doing so turns every possibility into an opportunity for failure and inhibits personal growth*
- *Learn to self-evaluate. Draw your own conclusions about your own behaviour, work, achievements and so on instead of relying exclusively on the opinion of others.*

The final words come from the women I have worked with over the years. The quotes below (and all the case studies) are true accounts of real situations. There is hope here for all of you – you can make the transition back to work and in doing so, fulfil your potential.

'I've realised that I can do much more than just be a full-time mum. I found my skills through writing a CV and I have more confidence now.'

'The greatest impact was having my confidence boosted in a very subtle way – being able to go back and connect to who I was in a younger time and sell my skills which I've had and have.'

'The course has helped me gain confidence and allowed me to realise I can actually do anything I set my mind to.'

'It has given me the foresight to take a risk and leave my comfort zone (not be scared to). It has helped both practically and mentally.'

'It has made me more aware of issues involved in returning to work. Though the time may not be right now, this has given me more direction for the future.'

'At the beginning of the course, I saw my life as my back garden – a bit untidy and with gaps. Now I see it as a garden

with potential – getting a shape and being luxuriant and interesting!'

In writing this book, I believe I have given you all the tools you need to make the transition from your current position to a working woman, if that is what you want. I hope you now feel ready for the challenge. The rest is up to you – good luck!

Appendix 1

Employment rights of women returning to work

**By Carolyn Brown LLB,
Employment Partner, Finers Stephens Innocent Solicitors**

INTRODUCTION

I shall assume throughout that you are a woman whose previous employment ended some considerable time earlier. Therefore the employment you start when you 'return' to work is the beginning of a new employment arrangement.

Returners with continuing service

If, instead, you are returning to work after either a period of maternity leave, as allowed by the general law, or following an agreed period of absence, the position will be different. Returners from a period of maternity leave are allowed by law to go back to their previous job or sometimes to a suitable alternative so that their continuity of employment is treated as unbroken.

Some other returners may have taken an agreed period of absence (often called a sabbatical) where continuity of length of service may be preserved through an agreement with the employer. Yet others may be entitled to re-start a job for which the terms have been agreed, possibly years in advance, but where they may not have been able to preserve their continuity of service.

Continuity of service can be very important since it gives the extra rights that are associated with long service, such as higher notice pay and more redundancy pay.

If you are returning to work after a period of statutory leave, such as parental leave, you are usually entitled to go back to your old job or, if that is no longer available, to a comparable role.

Returners as 'new recruits'

For all other returners, and these are the vast majority of those for whom this book is written, you will be making a fresh start at work and, in the eyes of the law, you are a new employee or worker.

The structure of this part of the book

I outline the rights and obligations of those starting new roles. Section A looks at this from the perspective of a woman returning to work and Section B considers the responsibilities as an employer which a woman returning to work has to her childcarer.

Section A begins with the setting up of the employment or work structure and explains the areas that should be covered in any written agreement. Then I explain the rights acquired with length of service and those which apply while the employment continues. I also deal with the right to return to work after short periods of absence while exercising the statutory right of an employee to take certain types of leave. Next I deal with the rights and obligations when employment comes to an end.

Finally, since many women returners become employers themselves of their childcarer when they return to work, I have added as Section B a short section on tips for the returner who is an employer, particularly of a nanny.

Changes in the law

The law concerning employment rights is constantly changing. I have stated the correct legal position as at 31 July 2003.

To help you to factor in any changes that happen subsequently, I have added to each section addresses for the very clear and influential Department of Trade and Industry (DTI) website on employment relations issues (*www.dti.gov.uk/er/*) and the ACAS website (*www.acas.org.uk*), which should contain up-to-date information. Please refer to these websites to check that the rights explained here remain current and to find any changes. It is very important to be up to date with your information because the exercise of your employment rights can often be time-critical.

Individual circumstances differ, so please do not rely on this book, which is intended for guidance only. Instead, make sure you get your own advice where you can, either from a solicitor, the Citizens' Advice Bureau (CAB) or Legal Advice Centre. If the work relationship goes wrong, you may be able to get help to bring a claim from some of the many schemes which give free or '*pro bono*' advice.

A: EMPLOYMENT RIGHTS OVERVIEW

People who work have two basic types of legal rights. The first type are the rights described in the employment contract (if you are an employee) or in the contract to provide services to your client (if you are self-employed). The second type are the additional rights you get automatically (or sometimes receive with length of service) under the law (of the UK or of Europe). These are called 'statutory rights'.

Work status – are you an employee or are you self-employed?

First and most importantly, find out whether you are going to be an employee or self-employed.

What is an employee? An employee works for a company or for another person according to a contract of employment. In general, the status of employee usually carries the most rights. The work the employee does and her working hours are specified by the employer. The employer deducts tax and National Insurance contributions before the employee is paid.

What does it mean to be self-employed? A woman who is self-employed either works for herself or is a partner with others in running a business that is not run through a company. The statutory rights of the self-employed are less than those of employees but, if you are self-employed, you are your own boss and you work when and how you choose. Self-employed workers are responsible for their own tax and National Insurance.

In the following sections, I will focus on employees' rights. The self-employed have very few of these but I will note where the self-employed are entitled to specific rights.

The contract of employment – what it must contain

Although the general law allows an employment contract to be made verbally or 'on a handshake' without any written document, you usually get a letter offering you the job. Often an employment contract is sent by the employer at the same time. Take care to read these documents carefully. To accept the offer of the job, you sign and return a copy of the offer letter and/or of the employment contract, or you write to the employer and accept the terms (if you are prepared to agree to them without any change). If the offer is not acceptable to you, try to negotiate changes until it is.

Offers of employment are often conditional on satisfactory references including one from a previous employer. Sometimes offers are dependent on a satisfactory medical. The offer letter will say if this is the case. There is no obligation to employ you unless and until the employer is satisfied about any conditions that apply. When the employer's offer is no longer conditional and it is accepted by you without any further changes being required, then you have made a binding employment contract.

In addition to the letter of offer and the employment contract, there is also often a staff handbook. This sets out the detail of the agreement and tells everyone how the employment relationship will operate in practice (*www.acas.org.uk/employment/et_epp.html*).

Whether or not you receive a document called an employment contract, it is also every employee's statutory right within two months of the employment starting to be given by their employer a written statement containing all of the following details:

- The name of the employer and the name of the employee
- The date the employment began
- The date the employee's continuous employment began (if you have had previous employment with this or with a connected employer sometimes the two periods of employment can be considered to be continuous)

This written statement must also give the details that applied not more than seven days before that statement is provided, covering:

- The scale of pay, the rate of pay, or the method of calculating pay
- The intervals at which you will be paid – e.g. weekly, monthly or otherwise
- The hours of work (including a statement of the normal working hours, if there are any)
- The entitlement to holidays including public/bank holidays and to holiday pay
- What provisions apply if the employee is unfit to work due to sickness or injury, including any sick-pay rights
- The right to a pension or to join a pension scheme
- The length of notice to be given by the employer to end the employment and the length of notice to be given by the employee if she wants to end the employment
- The job title or a brief description of the work
- If the employment is for a fixed period only, when it will end
- Either the place of work or, if the employee either has chosen to or can choose to work at various places, there must be both a statement giving the details of that right and the employer's (contact) address
- If there are agreements that affect the whole workforce in a

particular industry (such as trades union-negotiated arrangements) it should say that they apply to the employment

If the employee is going to be required to work outside the UK for
more than one month, the statement must also say:

- The period that is to be for
- The currency in which pay will be made while working outside
  the UK
- Any additional pay or benefits
- The terms and conditions that relate to returning to the UK

The employment contract – non-essentials

Often employment contracts cover other important areas such as
bonuses and benefits like private medical care, staff discounts, company pensions or share options.

Senior employees may be asked in their employment contract or
service agreement to agree after the employment ends not to work for
a rival business, and it is sensible to get legal advice if you are asked
to agree to this sort of complex provision.

Pay – how much and when

Once you have the job, the next most important issue is pay. The
employment contract will state how much you will be paid and when.
Most employees are paid monthly but some (such as nannies) receive
weekly pay. An employer is bound to provide each employee with a
pay statement showing the gross wage, deductions allowed or agreed
and the net amount. The dates, if any, for the review of pay may also
be stated in the employment contract.

Pay issues

I will outline four of the most common issues concerning pay.

Minimum rates: Pay must exceed the national minimum wage rate (of £4.50 per hour from October 2003 for adults aged 22 and over; see *www.dti.gov.uk/er/nmw/index.htm*). An employee's pay is usually stated as a gross sum which is the total figure. Tax and National Insurance are then deducted and a net sum is received.*

Deductions from pay or short pay: Retail workers have special rules limiting an employer's entitlement to make deductions for cash shortages or stock deficiencies to one tenth of gross wages. Otherwise, no employer may deduct sums from wages or pay short unless the employee has given her written agreement in advance to the deduction, or the employer is complying with a civil court judgment requiring it to make the deduction.

Sick pay: The period of any full or partial pay entitlement during sick leave will be explained in the employment contract. Employees qualify for statutory sick pay at a flat rate paid by the employer if they have four or more consecutive days sick leave (including Sundays and holidays) and the employer has been notified by them of their absence due to sickness.

An employee has to produce a self-certificate of sickness for the period of sickness absence for the period between the fourth and seventh consecutive day of any sickness absence and after seven consecutive days a doctor's certificate is required. After seven consecutive days sick leave, all sickness absence must be covered by a doctor's certificate.

The maximum entitlement to statutory sick pay in any period of three years is to 28 weeks pay at a flat rate (£75 per week in 2003).

Equal pay: Where a woman is involved in like work to a man, her contract is treated as including an entitlement to like pay with that comparable male worker. So, if men and women doing such comparable jobs do not receive equal pay, unless the employer can show the pay difference is for a reason other than her sex, the woman can claim from her employer the pay differential for up to the previous six

---

* Note that 'London Weighting' is an addition to the salary to take into account the higher cost of living in London.

years. To do this she would need to bring a claim before the Employment Tribunal.

Time off/working hours

There are a large number of entitlements to time off. Some rights will be specific to your employment contract, others apply to all employees, and yet others are acquired after a period of service. Some, such as maternity and paternity leave, are even gender-based.

There are also specific rules concerning the hours that you can be asked to work and when you must work them.

I will deal with the main rights.

Paid time off for holidays: All employees and some workers have a statutory right to four (working) weeks paid holiday over the 12-month period that each employer designates to be its holiday year. This statutory right is inclusive of bank holidays. This type of holiday also continues to accrue and can be paid for while an employee is on long-term sick leave.

Employment contracts often give employees an entitlement to more holiday than the statutory right – usually specified as a number of (working) days. Bank holidays are then often paid in addition to the holiday period stated in the contract and the contract will say if this is the case.

Part-timers get holiday entitlements scaled down by the proportion of a full week that they work – usually called pro-rata or pro-rated. Employers also have to ensure that part-timers do not lose out on their holiday rights as a result of the days on which they choose to work. For example, a woman who works on a Wednesday and Thursday has no guarantee of any paid bank holidays on her working days but someone working on a Monday and Friday would have at least four bank holidays falling on their working days in any year. Appropriate pay or leave adjustments should be made to compensate for such irregularities.

Paid rest breaks: After working for six hours continuously, an adult employee or self-employed worker is entitled to a rest break. Also, where an employee's work pattern may put health and safety at risk, in particular if work is monotonous or if the work rate is fixed in advance, more breaks may be necessary.

Time off for night workers: There are rules for breaks to be given to night workers and health assessments for night workers.

Time off for rest periods: Adults are entitled to a rest period of 11 consecutive hours in each 24-hour period and an uninterrupted rest period of at least 24 hours in each seven-day period of work.

Paid time off for working flexi-time: The employment contract will set out any arrangements which apply.

Maximum working hours each week: Employees and self-employed workers should not be required to work more than 48 hours each working week or as an average over a period of weeks. However, employees can agree in writing to work more than 48 hours but this should be done voluntarily. An employee can cancel this agreement to work more than 48 hours provided she gives written notice to the employer but that notice may need to be of up to three months in length. She has to continue to work the previous work pattern until that notice has expired.

The calculation of working hours includes time spent receiving training. Some jobs have what is called 'unmeasured work' and therefore longer hours may be required. Others have special rules (*www.dti.gov.uk/er/work time_regs/index.htm* and *www.acas.org.uk/q_a/q_a6.html*).

Paid time off to have children (maternity rights)

Ante-natal care: A pregnant employee must not be unreasonably refused time off during working hours to receive ante-natal care. For each appointment after the first the employer can ask to see a certificate from a doctor, midwife or health visitor confirming the employee is pregnant and to see an appointment card showing the appointment has been made.

Maternity leave/pay: All pregnant employees get 26 weeks maternity leave. They receive pay during that time but not at their usual pay rate. The first six weeks' maternity leave is paid at 9/10ths of normal weekly earnings (subject to a minimum) and the following 20 weeks' is paid at a flat rate (currently £100 per week from April 2003).

Employees with 26 weeks' continuous employment completed before the fourteenth week prior to the expected week of childbirth are entitled to an additional 26 weeks maternity leave. This is unpaid. This makes a total of 52 weeks' maternity leave before a woman has to return to work in order to keep her job.

Whatever other maternity leave is taken, no female employee is allowed to work in the two weeks following childbirth.

Some employee contractual benefits continue during the first 26 weeks of maternity leave but others do not. Few continue during the additional 26 weeks of maternity leave.

The self-employed may claim maternity allowance at a flat rate during some of their time off work due to childbirth (*www.dti. gov.uk/er/maternity.htm* and *www.dti.gov.uk/er/matleafr.htm*).

Paid time off for fathers when children are born (paternity leave)
Provided the male employee has 26 weeks' continuous service with that employer by the fifteenth week before the baby is due, there is a right to a block of one week or of two weeks or to two separate blocks of one week to be taken within 56 days of the date of the birth. They are paid at a flat rate (£100 per week from April 2003).

This paternity leave is available to a man with parental responsibility for the child or to the biological father or to the mother's husband or partner (*www.dti.gov.uk/er/paternity.htm*).

Paid time off for adoptive parents
Similar rights as for maternity and paternity leave and pay apply (*www.dti.gov.uk/er/adoption.htm* and *www.dti.gov.uk/er/individual/ adopt-p1515.htm*).

Unpaid time off for parenting (parental leave)

Provided they comply with the requirements as to prior notification, either a male or a female employee with one year's continuous service with that employer can take up to 13 weeks' unpaid leave per child (usually taken in blocks of four weeks per year) up until the child's fifth birthday (or age 18 if the child is disabled) if that employee has parental responsibility for a child.

There are special rules for a child born before 15 December 1999 whose fifth birthday is after that date. These specify that parental leave can be taken up to 30 March 2005.

The right is cumulative for each employee even if their employer changes (*www.dti.gov.uk/er/parental_leave.htm*).

Unpaid time off to support dependants (dependant care leave)

Employees must be allowed reasonable time off during working hours to support dependants. A dependant is their spouse, child, parent or a person who lives in the same household (except tenants, lodgers or boarders) and can include those who reasonably rely on the employee to make arrangements to provide care. This is time off to provide assistance when a dependant falls ill, gives birth, is injured or is assaulted.

It is also to make arrangements for care:

- For an ill or injured dependant
- Consequent on the death of the dependant
- Due to the unexpected disruption or termination of arrangements for the care of the dependant
- To deal with an incident concerning an employee's child when an educational establishment is caring for the child

It should be seen as an emergency leave period only and does not allow the employee to provide cover themselves except for cover over short periods for infant children.

Flexible working hours/choosing where to work

Employees with 26 weeks' service are entitled to request changes in the place where they work or the hours they work in order to assist them to care for a child under six. One request can be made each year.

Employers can only justify a refusal on valid grounds concerning the operation of the business and its clients' requirements (*www.dti.gov. uk/er/flexible.htm*, *www.dti.gov.uk/er/individual/flexible-p1516.htm* and *www.acas.org.uk/employment_et_fw.html*).

DISCRIMINATION RIGHTS – EMPLOYEES AND SELF-EMPLOYED WORKERS

Most rights to prevent discrimination or to claim compensation for discrimination apply both to employees and to the self-employed. This is a complex area and you should take specific advice if you believe you may have suffered discrimination.

Sex discrimination

A woman treated less favourably than a man, a married person treated less favourably than a single person, or an employee whose employer applies a provision, criterion or practice to a woman that the employer also applies to a man but which is:

- Such that it will be to the detriment of a considerably larger proportion of women than men
- Such that the employer cannot show it to be justifiable irrespective of the sex of the person to whom it is applied
- And is to the woman's detriment

is entitled to claim compensation for lost income as a result and a sum for damages for injury to her feelings.

Race discrimination

Employees and self-employed workers and applicants for jobs have similar rights in relation to discrimination on the ground of race or ethnic origin. A new right not to suffer discrimination on religious grounds should be in force from December 2004.

Disability discrimination

Unfavourable treatment on the ground of a disability entitles employees and job applicants to bring claims. Disabled employees are also entitled to require suitable adjustments to be made to working arrangements to facilitate their employment.

Part-time workers discrimination

A part-timer must not be treated less favourably than a comparable full-timer as regards:

- Pay and access to a company pension scheme
- Annual, maternity and parental leave
- Contractual sick pay
- Access to training

(*www.dti.gov.uk/er/ptime.htm*)

Fixed-term workers discrimination

Less favourable treatment of persons on a fixed-end-date employment contract is prohibited. Several fixed-term contracts following one another can convert to full-time employment (*www.dti.gov.uk/ er/fixed/index.htm*).

Sexual orientation discrimination

A new right prohibiting discrimination in relation to employment on the ground of sexual orientation should be in force from December 2003.

CONDUCT WHILE AT WORK

Employers will have policies requiring a certain level of personal behaviour in the workplace. These range from equal opportunities policies and anti-harassment policies through detailed policies on how and when you can take your contractual holiday to ones stating whom you should notify if you are sick and when you have to give that notification. They also cover issues such as the use of the company's IT and other systems for personal reasons (that is, non-business communications), whether such personal use is allowed at all, whether personal communications on office systems will be screened by the company and requiring your permission for any such screening. There will almost always be clear requirements to keep confidential your employer's business.

The penalty for contravening these policies will often be disciplinary proceedings. Disciplinary proceedings can lead to dismissal.

DISCIPLINE OR GRIEVANCE ISSUES

If the employer feels that the employee is not performing her duties to the required standard of competence or has committed an act of misconduct, the steps that the employer can take should be set out in a disciplinary policy. If employees are unhappy about work issues they should be able to raise a grievance.

From late 2004 each employment contract will be required to state the disciplinary and grievance policy that applies. The basic requirements will be that there should be no sanction for disciplinary matters and no decision on a grievance raised by an employee unless there has been a meeting with that employee about the issue.

At present grievances can only be raised by employees during employment. That also will change in 2004 to allow grievances to be raised after employment ends. There is positive encouragement to raise grievances before bringing tribunal claims and if a person refuses unreasonably to try to resolve an issue before resorting to a tribunal claim, they will be penalised.

No-one should be dismissed for a first breach of procedure or discipline unless it is very serious. (Serious breaches are usually called 'gross misconduct'.) Instead, a fair disciplinary process should be used. Any fair process will include:

- A fair investigation of the allegations
- The holding of a disciplinary meeting, with information having been given to the employee in advance of the charges and the factual allegations against her
- At any meeting the employee is entitled to be accompanied by a trades union representative or by a fellow worker
- A written note of the decision should be given to the employee

Always take care to put forward your side of the story honestly and thoroughly if you are called to a disciplinary meeting. The fellow employee or worker you are entitled to take with you to such a meeting can speak on your behalf but cannot answer questions for you.

So far as grievances are concerned, if an employee is dissatisfied with any aspect of her management or with the operation of her employment rights, she may complain by raising a formal grievance with her employer. The employer then has to investigate and respond to the employee.

CHANGES IN THE EMPLOYMENT RELATIONSHIP

Changes in employment contract terms must be notified to the employee usually at least a month in advance and should be clearly agreed. Failure by the employee to object to changes in terms may signify agreement in some cases.

If the employer sells the business, employees with one year's service are transferred with the business. If the employee's job disappears or the workplace closes, the employee's job may become redundant. So far as business transfers and redundancies are concerned, there are obligations to consult with employees both individually and collectively. There are financial penalties for failing to do so.

TERMINATION OF THE EMPLOYMENT CONTRACT

The employment can end in one of several ways:

- A fixed-term contract that comes to an end on its finish date. No notification or other notice is required by either party to end that type of employment contract since the contract ends automatically
- A termination by an employer on the ground of the employee's fault either by misconduct or poor performance. That is usually preceded by a disciplinary process and so an employee should be told what the problem is and given an opportunity to improve or remedy the fault before facing a dismissal unless the conduct is extremely serious
- By a notice to end the contract. The contract usually states how long this should be. Where the contract does not state the notice period, the employer must give one week's notice for each full year worked

Employees can terminate the contract by giving notice of resignation as required by the employment contract. If the contract does not state the notice period, an employee can leave on one week's notice but some more senior roles may have a longer period of notice assumed to apply – generally it will be the industry norm for that level of role.

Sometimes employees are asked to work their notice period and they have to do so if the employer wants them to. At other times they are paid in lieu of (instead of) working the notice period. Employers may breach the contract in such a fundamental way that it entitles the employee to leave.

REFERENCES

An employer has no obligation to give a reference for you unless you are moving jobs in a highly regulated industry where you cannot work without a clear reference from a former employer. An employer should answer any job reference request honestly. This means that they should not lie about you but also they cannot write in glowing terms about you if this would be misleading.

PENALTIES ON EMPLOYERS FOR UNFAIR DISMISSAL OR FOR BREACHES OF STATUTORY RIGHTS

As well as giving the period of notice specified in the contract or payment for that period, a dismissal by an employer has to be on one of five grounds and employers must act reasonably in order to avoid liability to their employees. The grounds are:

- Misconduct
- Lack of capability
- Redundancy
- That continuing of the employment would breach the general law
- Some other substantial reason

A failure to undergo a fair procedure and/or to have a fair reason could leave the employer liable to compensation for unfair dismissal. The maximum figure for a compensatory award for an unfair dismissal in 2003 is £53,500. You usually need to have one year's completed service by the time of termination to be able to bring a claim.

Other breaches of employee's statutory rights can entitle an employee to bring a separate claim or, if a breach is connected with the termination of employment, it can make that termination unfair and can give rise to an unfair-dismissal claim. Breaches of discrimination rights can also give rise to claims against employers and fellow workers. You do not need a qualifying period of service in a job before you can bring a discrimination claim.

Employees with concerns about regulatory issues or health and safety breaches should be given by their employer a confidential reporting line in order to notify employers of their concern and, if they are penalised by dismissal for doing so, employees are entitled to unlimited compensation for unfair dismissal.

B: BECOMING AN EMPLOYER YOURSELF

If you employ a nanny, either to live-in or as a daily, to look after your children when you return to work, you will become an employer. Remember, all the rights in Section A apply to your employee too.

Your nanny should be given an employment contract which should clearly set out the statutory particulars as to the terms and conditions of her employment. In the contract you should be clear and set out what you will pay for and how you will calculate the pay, sick pay and holidays. Add a job description with the details of her duties. If you want the nanny to keep a daily diary on what the children have done or eaten, specify this in the contract. State what she should do and what you will do. If you cannot afford to pay sick pay then say she will only get statutory sick pay. You should be careful about 'working time' issues and also make sure that pay rules are strictly followed and that proper tax treatment is given to her pay.

Again, your childcarer will be entitled to be paid during the statutory holiday period of four weeks inclusive of bank holidays and to be paid for any other holidays that you agree to give her.

Those employed as 'domestic servants in a private household', which arguably includes nannies, are exempt from the right only to work a 48-hour week and from night-work rights but some are entitled to rest periods and to time off for holidays. However, since many childcarers work more than 48 hours a week, you would be wise to ask them to sign a waiver of the working hours limit.

If your nanny is going to live-in, you should have a separate part of the agreement that deals with how she may use your home and your home benefits such as the TV, telephone, computers, car, kitchen and food.

You may be sharing a nanny with another family but she may still be your employee. She may then have two or three separate employments with different employers all at the same time.

If you are working with a childminder, she is probably self-employed and there may be a standard contract.

Be very careful about ending employment contracts. You have to give the agreed period of notice and, if she qualifies for the right not to be dismissed unfairly, you must be very careful indeed to check that you have a fair ground for that dismissal and that you do act fairly towards her. If you terminate a nanny's employment because she is pregnant, you could become liable to a claim by her for sex discrimination and for unfair dismissal.

If your childcarer is recently arrived from abroad, you need to check she is entitled to work in the UK.

Keep holiday records and give her pay statements.

Generally, remember that if your childcarer is your employee, she will probably be entitled to most of the rights that you get and that you expect from your employer and, what is more, she may be a returner herself!

Carolyn Brown
Finers Stephens Innocent Solicitors
179 Great Portland Street
London W1W 5LS
tel 020 7344 7667 or 020 7323 4000

Carolyn Brown is a solicitor and partner in the Employment Department of the central London law firm Finers Stephens Innocent Solicitors. She advises many large organisations on their obligations to their employees. She helps clients to understand their risk of claims by advising on employment law issues at good practice workshops for clients, and at other training events. She also broadcasts and writes articles on current employment topics. Carolyn has practised as a solicitor for 20 years and has two young children.

Appendix 2

Obligations as an employer of a nanny

By Sara Graff ACA ATII, Principal of Taxing Nannies

Employing a nanny brings with it the same obligations that any business has when taking on an employee. By law, therefore, an employer must account for income tax and National Insurance contributions on the salary paid to a nanny or mother's help, whether they are full-time, part-time or temporary, once the nanny is earning more than the weekly threshold of £89 per week. There are very few occasions when the Inland Revenue will accept that a nanny is self-employed, maternity nurses being an exception.

Avoiding the taxman is illegal. If the Revenue catches up with an employer who has failed to declare their nanny for tax purposes or has tried to maintain that she is self-employed, the employer will be liable to pay the correct tax and National Insurance contributions, and interest and penalties. There is no legal right to seek repayment from the nanny.

When a nanny is employed, it is the employer's obligation to open a PAYE scheme with the Inland Revenue and also to provide payslips for the nanny on a regular basis. The Inland Revenue will sometimes agree to set up a 'simplified' domestic PAYE scheme. This is not normally available where the nanny's taxable weekly pay is more than £160 or the taxable monthly pay is more than £700.

A nanny's salary is normally quoted net of deductions (i.e. the amount actually paid to the nanny), and it is therefore the employer's responsibility to pay over to the Inland Revenue the PAYE, Employee's National Insurance and Employer's National Insurance in addition to the net salary paid to the nanny. Expenses paid in benefits provided on behalf of a nanny in addition to her salary may be liable to a separate charge to tax and National Insurance.

Where an employer takes on a nanny as part of a nanny share the situation is more complicated and it will depend on the type of share as to whether the nanny has one joint employment or two (or more) separate employments. Where the nanny works for her employers at separate times, there will be two distinct employments. In such situations it is usual for the tax-free single person's allowance (for 2002/2003 £4,615 per annum) to be split proportionately between the employments so that the overall tax burden is divided equitably between the employers.

Employers are required to pay their nannies a salary at least equivalent to the national minimum wage. The current rates are a minimum gross wage of £4.50 per hour for employees aged 22 and over and £3.60 gross per hour for employees aged between 18 and 21. For live-in nannies an allowance of up to a maximum of £3.25 per day may be deducted from the nanny's salary in determining whether she is earning above the national minimum wage.

All full-time employees are entitled to a minimum of four weeks annual holiday (including bank holidays) in accordance with the provisions of the working time directive. Part-time employees are entitled to the same holiday entitlement pro rata.

An employer is normally obliged to pay Statutory Sick Pay (SSP) and Statutory Maternity Pay (SMP) to the nanny when applicable, although in the case of SMP the gross amount payable is fully recoverable in advance from the Inland Revenue together with an additional 4.5 per cent. SSP is often also recoverable but the calculation is complicated and depends on each individual case.

Other matters that an employer may need to consider are tax credits, which are sometimes required to be administered via the payroll, and student loan deductions. In both cases the Inland Revenue will inform an employer when such adjustments to the nanny's pay are required.

Sara Graff ACA ATII is principal of Taxing Nannies, a specialist payroll agency for employers of nannies (see page 203; call them on 020 8882 6847 for further information and updates). Sara is the mother of two children and has employed nannies herself while continuing her career.

Appendix 3

Rejoining the workplace – a financial guide

Tax and National Insurance issues

By Sharon Nash ATT, Tax Associate, Frenkels Chartered Accountants

If you are rejoining the workplace after a period of time away, you will find that there have been some considerable changes to the taxation system. A major change happened in 1996/97 when the Government introduced the self-assessment tax regime. You may find that some things are unchanged – such as handing in a P45 when you start a new job – and some are completely new to you – like the requirement to complete a self-assessment return if you have a reportable tax liability. In what follows I hope to remind you of procedures that were once familiar to you and inform you of new procedures.

A. WORKING FOR SOMEONE ELSE

I will start by addressing women who were married or widowed prior to 6 April 1977 and elected to pay the reduced-rate National Insurance contributions. Provided that:

- Your marriage has not ended in divorce or annulment
- You have not remarried, if a widow at 6 April 1977
- You have not had a two-year continuous break from paying

157

National Insurance contributions, either as an employed or self-employed person

you may either continue to pay at the reduced rate or opt to pay at the full rate. By electing to pay full-rate contributions you will increase your entitlement to social security benefits and National Insurance retirement pension. Brochure CA13 (*National Insurance Contributions for Women with Reduced Elections*) is available from the Inland Revenue outlining your choices and the advantages of changing your election. Inland Revenue phone numbers are available either from the telephone directory under Inland Revenue, directory enquiries or online (*www.inlandrevenue.gov.uk*; pamphlets and forms may be downloaded from this website). To assist you in making any decisions you may seek advice from an independent financial adviser (IFA). He or she will advise you regarding your pension entitlement and contributions.

Legislation changes mean that women married after 5 April 1977 are no longer given the option to pay reduced-rate contributions, nor can a retrospective election be made. Single women and those co-habiting with a partner are required to pay the full-rate contributions. Separated and divorced women lost their entitlement to pay at the reduced rate on the break-up of their marriage and are required to pay at the full rate.

To continue paying reduced-rate National Insurance contributions, you must supply your employer with a valid CA4139 (CF383) or CF380A, allowing you to pay at the reduced rate. Without this certificate your employer is obliged to deduct standard-rate contributions. If you have lost your certificate you may apply for a duplicate by completing form CF9, which is supplied with pamphlet CA13 referred to above.

Irrespective of your marital status, when you start work your new employer will need some documents from you:

- A P45 (Certificate of Employee Leaving) from your last employment. If you no longer have the form or it is out of date, then your employer will ask you to complete a P46 (Notice of New Employee). Completing the form fully and accurately will result in the correct tax deductions being made by your employer. To

ensure that any National Insurance contributions are properly credited to you, quote your correct NI number on the form
• Your bank or building society details if you want your salary to be paid directly into your account

If you earn more than the National Insurance and/or PAYE thresholds, your employer will deduct tax on an emergency code until such time as the Inland Revenue processes the P45 or P46 and issues your personal tax code. Dealing with correspondence promptly will speed up the process.

During the course of your employment your employer will provide you with certain forms, which you need to retain:

• A P60 (Certificate of Pay and Tax) recording your income, tax and National Insurance paid for each tax year
• A P9 or P11D (Expenses and Benefits) recording any reimbursed expenses and benefits provided to you by virtue of your employment. You will only receive a form if your employer provides such benefits to you
• A P45 (Certificate of Employee Leaving) – when you leave an employment

B. WORKING FOR YOURSELF

If you start in business you must advise:

• The Inland Revenue National Insurance Office
• Your local Inspector of Taxes
• Customs and Excise, if your taxable turnover (total sales) is more than £56,000 (10 April 2003 rate)
• Your Job Centre, if you are registered with one

National Insurance

If you have lost your National Insurance number, either your local Contributions Agency or Inland Revenue office should be able to trace it for you using your date of birth. Phone numbers are available either from the telephone directory under Inland Revenue, directory enquiries, or online (www.inlandrevenue.gov.uk).

As a self-employed person you are liable to pay two classes of contributions:

- Class 2 National Insurance **and**
- Class 4 National Insurance based on taxable profits

Class 2 National Insurance contributions: These are flat-rate contributions that are usually paid by direct debit. The rate for 2003/04 is £2 per week. If your earnings are below £4,095 there is no obligation to pay, as you will be covered by the small earnings exemption.

Class 4 National Insurance Contributions: You will pay these (in addition to Class 2 contributions) if your profits exceed a limit announced annually in the Budget. For 2003/04, Class 4 is payable on profits (income less any business expenses) in the range of £4,615–£30,940 at 8 per cent and on profits above £30,940 at 1 per cent. The liability is determined when you complete your annual accounts (see Income Tax, below).

If, due to the level of your income, you are not required to pay National Insurance contributions, you may choose to pay a voluntary contribution (which at April 2003 is £6.95 per week) to protect your entitlement to certain benefits. You should note that not all benefits are protected and your local Department for Work and Pensions can advise you fully about this. Phone numbers are available from your telephone directory, directory enquiries and online (*www.dwp.gov.uk*).

Income Tax

The Inland Revenue require you to advise them when you start in business. Under self-assessment legislation, you have until 30 October in the year following the commencement of your business to advise the Inspector, otherwise penalties will apply. It is advisable to notify the Inland Revenue immediately you start in business to avoid such penalties, and allow you time to complete any necessary forms the Inspector sends to you. Make a note of the ten-digit tax reference used by the Inspector – that reference is unique to you and should be used for all correspondence with the Inspector and on personal tax payments. It is always advisable to keep copies of correspondence and forms in case of later problems, and always ensure that your tax reference and/or National Insurance number are quoted fully on correspondence that you send to the Inspector. Especially ensure that your reference is shown on the reverse of any cheques that you send to the Collector of Taxes.

You may decide to appoint an accountant who will advise you about:

- Which accounting date to choose
- Preparation of accounts and book-keeping
- Tax, VAT and National Insurance payable

Should you decide to deal with your own affairs, then you have a statutory obligation to complete documentation for the Government. Depending on the way in which you operate your business, all or some of the following will be required:

- An annual self-assessment return – reporting your income, gains and claims for each fiscal year
- An annual partnership return – if you are trading in partnership
- VAT returns dependent on your quarterly turnover
- P35s (end-of-year summary), P14s (record of annual earnings), P9 and/or PIIDs (report of benefits and expenses provided to employees) and statistical reports for National Statistics Office – if you employ staff

Value Added Tax (VAT)

VAT is added to most goods and services provided. Almost any business transaction can constitute a 'taxable supply' for VAT purposes. Some types of supply are 'exempt supplies', such as financial and educational services. Certain types of goods are generally zero-rated; these include children's clothes and food. The current standard rate is 17.5 per cent on all services and goods that are not exempt or zero-rated.

- You may voluntarily register for VAT if your business turnover does not exceed the registration limit of £56,000 (in 2003/04). This may be beneficial if your customers are registered for VAT
- You *must* register for VAT if your annual business turnover exceeds (or is likely to exceed) £56,000
- If you register you *must* charge output tax (17.5 per cent VAT) on taxable supplies to your customers
- You must then complete VAT returns
- There are several VAT schemes to choose from and the timing of VAT payments depend on the choice of scheme
- You may offset against the output tax charged to your customers any input tax charged to you by your suppliers
- If the VAT paid on your sales is less than that paid on your purchases you may reclaim the difference – if not then you pay the excess to Customs and Excise

Becoming an employer (other than for domestic staff)

Employing staff means that you have a statutory obligation to advise your local tax office that you have become an employer. In response to this notification you will receive a New Employer's Pack providing all the tables and documents you need to operate the PAYE (Pay as You Earn) scheme and deduct tax and National Insurance at the current rates. The tables and forms provided enable you to:

- Calculate the amount of tax and National Insurance your employee has to pay
- Calculate the amount of employer's National Insurance you have to pay
- Calculate any statutory maternity or sick pay
- Record these payments on form P11 (Deductions Working Sheet)
- Provide the Inland Revenue with documentation relevant to your

employee; for example, P46 (Notification of New Employee) and P45 (Details of Employee Leaving)

Remember that you may also be required to:

- Make appropriate deductions if required to do so for an attachment of earnings or for student loan repayments
- Pay tax credits on receipt of instructions from the Tax Credit Agency

Separately, you will receive a payslip booklet and a supply of pre-paid addressed envelopes for you to send to the Collector of Taxes with the deductions that you make. You must send the amount deducted during the month to the Collector of Taxes by the 19th of the following month; e.g. payments deducted in June 2003 should be paid over by 19 July 2003. Some small employers (for 2003 this is determined by your average monthly payments not exceeding £1,500) are allowed to pay amounts over quarterly rather than monthly. Ask the Collector of Taxes if you qualify and if so he will note your records and prevent monthly reminders being issued. You can obtain their phone number from the telephone directory under Inland Revenue Collector of Taxes, directory enquiries or online (*www.inlandrevenue.gov.uk*).

As an employer, at the end of each financial year you are required to complete the following summary documentation:

- P14s (end-of-year summary) – this is a three-part form. Two copies are sent to the Inland Revenue and one part, labelled P60, must be handed to your employee
- P35 (employer's annual return) – summarises total tax and National Insurance, both employee's and employer's, for the tax year just ended
- P9D and P11D (expenses and benefits provided) – reports any reimbursed expenses and benefits that you have provided to your staff during the year

Your local tax office may be able to provide details of free courses they have organised to help new employers to gain a better understanding of their new responsibilities.

Alternatively if you would rather someone else dealt with the payroll for you, approach a local payroll bureau, book-keeping agency or accountant, any of which will provide you with a quote for undertaking this work on your behalf.

C. PENSIONS

The provisions for making pensions contributions have undergone some major changes in recent years. New legislation comes into force in April 2004, which it is hoped will simplify what has become a complex area.

If you are employed and invited to join your employer's pension scheme you will obtain tax relief on the contributions that you make through the payroll. If you are not in pensionable employment or are self-employed you need to consider setting up a personal pension scheme. Numerous choices exist, all of which provide basic tax relief at source (i.e. you make your contribution net of basic rate tax but you receive credit for the gross amount). If you pay tax at the higher rate, any additional tax relief on pension contributions must be claimed on your self-assessment tax return.

Many companies, banks, building societies, and financial institutions offer pension policies; you may even find details at your supermarket. However, it may be advisable to seek professional help, especially if you have existing pension policies and need to know if they are suitable to transfer into your new scheme.

You may need to speak to an Independent Financial Adviser (IFA). If you do not know one yourself, speak to your accountant or solicitor for a recommendation, or consult the list of IFAs in the telephone directory. Normally, IFAs will not charge you for taking out a policy as they are paid commission direct from the policy provider. If, however, your affairs are more complicated and you require a detailed financial plan, then the IFA will advise you in advance and give you an estimate of the fees involved.

IFAs can also advise you about whether it will be advantageous for you to opt out of SERPS (State Earnings Related Pension Scheme) and about opting to pay full-rate National Insurance contributions (see the section covering National Insurance, above).

Before making any decision about a personal pension policy you may wish to check your existing entitlement to the State Retirement Pension. This may also be relevant if you think that you might not have received full credit for the National Insurance that you have paid to date. To obtain a pension forecast, you should contact the Retirement Pension Forecast Team – their office is open for calls Monday to Friday, 8.00am–8.00pm and Saturday, 9.00am–1.00pm. If you use the number given below your call will be charged at a local rate.

Pension Service
R.P.F.T.
Tyne View Park
Newcastle Upon Tyne
NE98 1BA
Telephone: 0845 3000168

D. WORKING TAX CREDITS AND CHILDREN'S TAX CREDITS

Working tax credit is for people in paid work who have a relatively low income (for couples, joint income), including those with a disability. It replaces adult-related elements of Working Families' Tax Credit and Disabled Person's Tax Credit. It also includes support for the cost of eligible childcare.

Working Tax Credit is for people who are employed or self-employed (either on their own or in partnership) who:

- Usually work 16 hours or more a week
- Are paid for that work
- Expect to work for at least four weeks

And who are:

- Aged 16 or over and responsible for at least one child, or
- Aged 16 or over and disabled, or
- Aged 25 or over and usually work at least 30 hours a week

Entitlement to tax credits is initially based on income for the previous year and, if you are part of a couple, is based on your combined income from all sources. At the end of the tax year, when your income for the year is known, the tax credits position is reviewed and any adjustment made.

A claim for tax credits cannot be backdated for more than three months, so if you think that you may be entitled, the sooner that you claim the better. Even if you are not currently entitled to make a claim it may be worthwhile making a protective claim to establish your entitlement for a complete year should your circumstances change.

SOME USEFUL LINKS

- National Insurance – *www.inlandrevenue.gov.uk/nic/*
- VAT – *www.hmce.gov.uk*
- Inland Revenue – *www.inlandrevenue.gov.uk*
- Working Tax Credit – *www.inlandrevenue.gov.uk/menus/credits.htm*

If you have any worries or concerns help is always available. If you have an accountant, he or she will advise you about any National Insurance, income tax or VAT issues. Alternatively, the relevant Government departments will help and advise you free of charge.

Sharon Nash ATT, Tax Associate
Frenkels Chartered Accountants
Frontier House
Merchants Quay
Salford Quays
Manchester M50 3SR
tel 0161 886 8080
fax 0161 886 8081
e-mail *sharon.nash@frenkels.com*
www.frenkels.com

Sharon Nash has over 30 years' experience of UK taxation, having worked for both the Inland Revenue and in private practice, and has a wealth of knowledge and experience in advising clients on tax-related issues. She is a member of the Association of Tax Technicians and is part of Frenkels Chartered Accountants' tax team. Outside work Sharon is studying with the Open University for a Humanities degree and is married with a married daughter.

A directory of organisations

While this does not claim to be a comprehensive list of organisations, it is as up-to-date as possible and provides a representative selection relevant to readers of this book. If readers feel that there are significant omissions or would like to give us information on updates, please e-mail *dianawolfin@changingdirection.com*.

A. WOMEN'S ORGANISATIONS

Aviva
41 Royal Crescent
London W11 4SN
fax 020 7371 6315
e-mail *kateb@aviva.org*
www.aviva.org
An international feminist website providing information and news on women's rights worldwide, listing women's organisations, resources and events.

Black Women Mean Business (BWMB)
PO Box 11371
Stoke Newington
London N16 8TY
tel 020 7219 4426
e-mail *carbye@parliament.uk*
An initiative launched by Diane Abbott MP in 1993. She started the organisation as a way of helping black women business owners to

develop the skills and expertise needed to become successful entrepreneurs. Initially BWMB consisted of professionals based within her constituency in Hackney, but now it has members from across London and from other parts of the UK. It is a non-profit-making organisation. Each year it hosts an annual reception for members as well as smaller workshops, seminars and specific one-off events, all with the aim of encouraging networking, sharing information and enhancing business acumen.

Corona Worldwide (Women's Corona Society)
Southbank House
Black Prince Road
London SE1 7SJ
tel 020 7793 4020
fax 020 7793 4042
e-mail *hq@coronaww.prestel.co.uk*
www.coronaworldwide.freeserve.co.uk
Support and advice group for expatriate women, formed in 1950. Supports people going to work and live in other countries, and also those coming to live in Britain, giving them information on living conditions here.

European Federation of Black Women Business Owners
2 Tunstall Road
London SW9 8DA
tel 020 7978 9488
fax 020 7987 9490
e-mail *yvonne.thompson@asapcomms.co.uk*
www.efbwbo.net
Launched in October 1996 and now has more than 4,000 members in the UK, France, Belgium and Holland. Holds an annual conference with workshops and makes awards as well as providing networking opportunities and support for minority businesses.

Everywoman.co.uk
tel 0870 746 1800
e-mail *info@everywoman.co.uk*
www.everywoman.co.uk
Provides products and services to assist women to start and run their businesses. The website is a comprehensive online resource giving women business owners access to free information and advice. **Every-woman's Business on the Move** conference programme provides a forum for learning and networking at regional and national level.

The Fawcett Society
1–3 Berry Street
London EC1V 0AA
tel 020 7253 2598
fax 020 7253 2599
e-mail *info@fawcettsociety.org.uk*
www.fawcettsociety.org.uk
www.equalcitizen.org.uk
The UK's leading organisation campaigning for equality between women and men. Its vision is of a society in which women and men are equal partners in the home, at work and in public life. Fawcett is a membership organisation offering supporters the opportunity to take practical action to make a difference to women's lives.

Global Women Innovators and Inventors Network (GWIIN)
4 Waverley Gardens
Barking
Essex IG11 0BQ
tel 020 8591 9964
fax 020 8594 2811
e-mail *office@gwiin.com*
www.gwiin.com
Promotes the work of women in this field. It holds a conference, promotes education for children, makes awards and gives advice. GWIIN also holds exhibitions focusing on the importance of intellectual property rights and international trade.

National Association of Women's Clubs
5 Vernon Rise
King's Cross Road
London WC1X 9EP
tel 020 7837 1434
fax 020 7713 0727
e-mail *nawc@tinyworld.co.uk*
www.nawc.org.uk
Promotes education and recreational facilities or other leisure activities for women. Holds an annual conference, meetings and workshops, and issues a newsletter.

National Council of Women (NCW)
36 Danbury Street
London N1 8JU
tel 020 7354 2395
fax 020 7354 9214
e-mail *ncwgb@danburystreet.freeserve.co.uk*
www.ncwgb.org
Founded in 1895, to provide a forum for women workers. Its current agenda includes social inclusion, quality of life, sustainable development, genetically modified agriculture and biotechnology, trafficking in women, consumer rights, employment, equality, pensions, women's health issues, violence against women and children, and the welfare of the family. Research is undertaken on a wide range of topics and branches countrywide offer opportunities to meet other women for discussion and debate. There is an annual conference.

National Federation of Women's Institutes (NFWI)
104 New Kings Road
London SW6 4LY
tel 020 7371 9300
e-mail *hq@nfwi.org.uk*
www.womens-institute.org.uk
The largest national voluntary organisation for women in England and Wales with around 230,000 members in around 7,300 WIs. NFWI is an educational, social, non-party-political and non-sectarian organisation. NFWI's work includes education and training, campaigning

and public affairs, and WI enterprises. It campaigns on social issues, health, food, education, the environment and international affairs.

Prowess
Lion House
20–28 Muspole Street
Norwich NR3 1DJ
tel 01603 762355
fax 01603 227090
e-mail *admin@prowess.org.uk*
www.prowess.org.uk
Trade association for organisations committed to providing women-friendly business support. The Prowess website has map-based links to locally based women-friendly business support providers across the UK and also inspirational stories of ordinary women who have started their own businesses.

Rights of Women
52–54 Featherstone Street
London EC1Y 8RT
tel 020 7490 2562; advice line 020 7251 6577 (Tuesday to Thursday, 14.00–16.00; Friday, 12.00–14.00)
fax 020 7490 5377
e-mail *info@row.org.uk*
www.rightsofwomen.org.uk
Works to attain justice and equality by informing, educating and empowering women on their legal rights. Advice line gives free legal advice for and by women and provides downloadable information sheets and training for organisations on women's rights. Also information on current research projects.

The 300 Group
PO Box 166
Horsham RH13 9YS
tel 01403 733797
e-mail *300group@horsham.co.uk*
www.300group.org.uk
Aims for a minimum 300 women Members of Parliament and

encourages women to seek public office and participate in the decision-making process at all levels. Web page lists public appointments available; this is a service offered to members since 1997. It offers a practical approach to the aim of encouraging women to participate in public life.

Townswomen's Guilds
4th floor, Chamber of Commerce House
75 Harborne Road
Edgbaston
Birmingham B15 3DA
tel 0121 456 3435 (central hotline)
fax 0121 452 1890
e-mail *tghq@townswomen.org.uk*
www.townswomen.org.uk
Guilds are groups of women who meet regularly to exchange ideas, develop skills and interests and debate various issues. The Townswomen's Guilds were formed in 1928 and hold national conferences, and regional monthly meetings. They issue a quarterly magazine and other publications on matters of interest such as long-term care and personal safety for women.

Women in Docklands
Chair: Heather Waring
tel 020 8220 6919
e-mail *heather@waringwell.com*
Non-profit organisation set up in 1991 as a network for business women working or living in Docklands in East London. It welcomes business women from all areas of the capital and beyond, who wish to expand their contacts in the region. Members range from sole traders to women in senior-level corporate posts, from the public, private and voluntary sectors.

Women Returners' Network in Association with the Grow Trust
Chelmsford College
Moulsham Street
Chelmsford CM2 0JQ
tel 01245 263796 (helpline)

e-mail *contact@women-returners.co.uk*
www.women-returners.co.uk
A national charity dealing with issues concerning women returners. Its aim is to provide innovative and practical support with a genuine 'hands-on' role to meeting the needs of its clients. It provides a helpline for women who need advice and guidance.

Women's Environmental Network
PO Box 30626
London E1 1TZ
tel 020 7481 9004
fax 020 7481 9144
e-mail *info@wen.org.uk*
www.wen.org.uk
National membership charity educating, informing and empowering women and men who care about the environment. Has a network of local groups and campaigns on environment and health links, food and composting, real nappies, sanitary protection and waste prevention.

B. PROFESSIONAL ASSOCIATIONS

This list summarises associations and special-interest groups representing professional women, but it is not intended to be a comprehensive list of more general professional associations, for which readers are advised to consult the current editions of the long-standing *CBD: Directory of British Associations* or the *Aslib Directory of Information Sources in the UK*. Both should be in public reference libraries.

Association for Women in Science and Engineering (AWISE)
59 Portland Place
London W1N 3AJ
e-mail *info@awise.org*
www.awise.org
Administrator: Dr Nina Baker
1636 Great Western Road

Glasgow G13 1HH
tel 0141 954 4602
fax by arrangement
e-mail *bakerwhitelaw@care4free.net*
National organisation established in 1994 as a support network, forum, and centre of resource and information for women in SET (science, engineering and technology), promoting SET for women and girls. AWISE works with government and the media, and a range of women's organisations here and overseas.

Association of Women in Property
tel 020 7603 4746
fax 020 7603 2818
e-mail *f.alfred@btinternet.com*
www.wipnet.org
Provides a dynamic forum for the professional development of women in the property and construction industry – to enhance business opportunities, exchange views, network and gain knowledge.

Association of Women Solicitors
The Law Society
114 Chancery Lane
London WC2A 1PL
tel 020 7320 5793
e-mail *enquiries@womensolicitors.org.uk*
www.lawsociety.org.uk
Works to promote the professional and business interests of women solicitors.

British Association of Women Entrepreneurs (BAWE)
Suite F, 123–125 Gloucester Place
London W1H 3SB
tel 020 7935 0085
fax 020 7486 6016
e-mail *woutersz@aol.com*
www.bawe-uk.org
Non-profit organisation affiliated to Les Femmes Chefs d'Entreprises Mondiales (FCEM). Founded in 1954 to encourage personal

development of members and to provide opportunities for them to grow their businesses through networking, the BAWE website focuses on marketing and advertising, trade missions and conferences, mentoring and training, and information exchange via the net.

British Federation of Women Graduates (BFWG)
2 Mandeville Courtyard
142 Battersea Park Road
London SW11 4NB
tel/fax 020 7498 8037
e-mail *info@bfwg.org.uk*
www.bfwg.org.uk
Promotes women's opportunities in education and public life and works as part of an international organisation to improve the lives of women and girls. Members automatically belong to the International Federation of University Women and University Women of Europe. BFWG offers an opportunity to meet like-minded women, to participate in various activities including study groups, lobbying government and networking. Scholarships are awarded to women final year PhD students.

Chartered Management Institute
Management House
Cottingham Road
Corby
Northants NN17 1TT
tel 01536 204222
fax 01536 401013
e-mail *mic.enquiries@managers.org.uk*
www.managers.org.uk
Formed in 1992 by the merger of the British Institute of Management and the Institution of Industrial Managers, it became the Chartered Management Institute in 2002. It is the UK's leading organisation for professional management and has members, both individual and corporate, from all sectors, public and private. It offers members access to and advice on management training and development programmes, courses, CV and career fact sheets, networking opportunities and a range of professional journals and publications.

Chartered Institute of Personnel & Development (CIPD)
CIPD House
Camp Road
Wimbledon
London SW19 4UX
tel 020 8263 3311
fax 020 8263 3250
e-mail *careers@cipd.co.uk*
www.cipd.co.uk
The IPD was formed by the amalgamation some years ago of the former Institute of Personnel Management and former Institute of Training & Development; it received chartered status in 2000. It is a centre of excellence in setting standards in management and people development, and, with a membership of over 118,000, is the largest single organisation in Europe representing professionals working in people management. The CIPD website provides information on employment law and bills in progress, and also offers a legal advisory service.

Daphne Jackson Trust
Trust Director: Jenny Woolley
Fellowship Administrator: Sue Smith
tel 01483 689 166
e-mail *djmft@surrey.ac.uk*
www.daphnejackson.org
Charitable organisation that helps women and men retrain and return to science, engineering and technology careers in both academia and industry, after a break due to family commitments. Two-year part-time paid fellowships are awarded, during which the fellows are able to work on a research project, retrain and learn new skills to enable them to find work. The trust runs the country's foremost returner's scheme and has awarded over 100 fellowships with a 98-per-cent success rate for returning scientists.

International Stress Management Association UK
PO Box 348
Waltham Cross
EN8 8ZL
tel 07000 780430
e-mail *stress@isma.org.uk*
www.isma.org.uk
Registered charity with a multi-disciplinary professional membership.
It exists to promote sound knowledge and best practice in the prevention and reduction of human stress. It sets professional standards for the
benefit of individuals and organisations using its members' services.

Medical Women's Federation (MWF)
Tavistock House North
Tavistock Square
London WC1H 9HX
tel 020 7387 7765
fax 020 7388 9216
e-mail *mwf@btconnect.com*
www.mwfonline.org.uk
Works to change discriminatory attitudes and practices and achieve
equality in the medical workforce. It holds national conferences,
involves members in monitoring and planning changes in women's
health services and presses for family-friendly employment policies
and childcare tax relief. There are local associations, a newsletter and
financial assistance for women medical students and doctors in need.
The federation is represented on major committees of the DoH, BMA,
royal colleges and other national and international medical bodies.

National Association of Women Pharmacists (NAWP)
e-mail *enquiries@nawp.org.uk*
www.nawp.org.uk
An independent organisation representing women in the profession of
pharmacy. Its aim is to help all women pharmacists to realise their full
potential and raise their profile by being educationally, socially and
politically active. It runs a weekend conference which 'provides a
unique learning atmosphere that is both friendly and reassuring,
especially to those who need to regain or restore their confidence, as

well as their competence to practise, after a career break or change in an increasingly demanding profession'. Local branches offer fellowship with other pharmacists and organise informal meetings with guest speakers. There are also opportunities for networking and mentoring.

Royal Society of Chemistry (RSC), Women Members Network
Thomas Graham House
Science Park
Milton Road
Cambridge CB4 0WF
tel 01223 432267
fax 01223 432133
e-mail *viney@rsc.org*
www.rsc.org; www.chemsoc.org
The number of women members of the RSC has increased from 4,000 in 1988 to 8,400 in 1998. The society is committed to developing and implementing services, facilities and programmes of activity relevant to the scientific and professional needs of women in the chemical sciences, and actively promotes the entry and re-entry of women to the profession. There are 19 regional networks currently running in the UK; they usually hold three meetings a year, which vary from simple social events (either in the home or at a local restaurant) to lectures on professional development or a broader scientific topic.

Trade Association Forum
Centre Point
103 New Oxford Street
London WC1A 1DU
tel 020 7395 8283
fax 020 7395 8178
www.taforum.org
Encourages development and sharing of best practice among UK trade associations. The website provides information about UK trade associations and business sectors and the directory lists associations, guilds or federations by industry or organisation name.

WITEC (European Database of Women Experts in Science, Engineering and Technology)
9 Emily Road
Sheffield S7 1HH
tel/fax 0114 220 7127
e-mail *witec@inovaconsult.com*
European network with co-ordinators in 14 European countries. It is hosted by Inova Consultancy and is funded by EU and national funding bodies to undertake projects that aim to redress the balance of women studying and working in science, engineering and technology. WITEC aims to increase the number of girls and women studying SET subjects and help them progress to related careers, to develop women's technical and entrepreneurial skills through training initiatives and projects, to create networking opportunities for women in SET and promote and support research into areas relating to women in non-traditional fields.

Women and Manual Trades (WAMT)
52–54 Featherstone Street
London EC1Y 8RT
tel 020 7251 9192
fax 020 7251 9193
e-mail *info@wamt.org*
www.wamt.org
Encourages women to train and work in the area of manual trades, particularly in the construction industry, working with projects to promote good practice in employment.

Women Building London
tel 0800 634 0165
e-mail *info@womenbuildinglondon.org*
www.womenbuildinglondon.org
A flagship development by Women's Education in Building, Women Building London offers advice on the construction industry, choosing a trade and setting up your own business. It also offers a career action plan, training and qualifications, work experience and job prospects.

Women in Banking and Finance (WIBF)
43 Keswick Road
West Wickham
Kent BR4 9AS
tel 020 8777 6902
fax 020 8777 7064
e-mail *wibf_ann@btopenworld.com*
www.wibf.org.uk
Non-profit-making networking group founded in 1980 and sponsored by banks and city institutions. It aims to empower its members in the banking and finance industry to realise their full potential. WIBF provides a Personal Excellence Programme (incorporating personal development, mentoring and coaching, media and presentation skills and professional development), Networking Beyond Boundaries and a senior executive programme. An Awards for Achievement lunch, annual address and Speaker Series give access to leaders in the banking and finance industry. WIBF publishes a bimonthly newsletter and the above programmes are currently available in both London and Scotland.

Women In Business for Merseyside
e-mail *ellen.kerr@womeninbusiness.co.uk*
www.womeninbusiness.co.uk
Network that brings together and supports women in business, management, the professions and education and facilitates networking opportunities. Also provides business-relevant workshops. Launched in 1994 for women in the north-west.

Women in Film and Television (WFTV UK)
6 Langley Street
Covent Garden
London WC2H 9JA
tel 020 7240 4875
fax 020 7379 1625
e-mail *info@wftv.org.uk*
www.wftv.org.uk
Founded in 1990 and is a membership organisation open to women with at least one year's professional experience in the film, television

and digital new media industries. Membership covers a wide range from senior executives to writers, producers, actresses, accountants, directors, composers, etc. It aims to provide information and career support for members, offer an educational forum, promote and safeguard the interests of women in the industry, and champion women's achievements. Events include workshops, screenings, networking opportunities, discussions and a variety of talk formats. A directory of members is available online to members only.

Women in Music
7 Tavern Street
Stowmarket
Suffolk IP14 1PJ
tel 01449 673990
fax 01449 673994
e-mail *info@womeninmusic.org.uk*
www.womeninmusic.org.uk
Helps to raise public awareness of women's work in all types of music. Projects include a commissioning fund and a professional development scheme. Founded 1987.

Women in Publishing (WiP)
e-mail *info@wipub.org.uk*
www.wipub.org.uk
Has offered networking, training and mutual support to women in publishing since 1979. It aims to help women in all areas of the publishing industry through a regular programme of meetings where members can share information and expertise. Members have access to the monthly online newsletter, *WiPlash*.

Women into Computing
Department of Computer Science
University of Keele
Keele
Staffs ST5 5BG
tel 01782 583 077
fax 01782 713 082
e-mail *a.f.grundy@cs.keele.ac.uk*

www.wic.org.uk
Founded in October 1988, a network of people committed to raising the profile of women in the fields of computing and IT. With overseas members and people from many different areas of computing, it holds conferences, seminars, discussion groups and other events, and issues a newsletter.

Women's Engineering Society (WES)
22 Old Queen Street
London SW1H 9HP
tel 020 7233 1974
e-mail *info@wes.org.uk*
www.wes.org.uk
Founded in 1919, WES is an organisation for all those interested in engineering, whether students, practising engineers, engineers taking a career break or retired. It publishes a quarterly journal, holds an annual conference and there are informal circles locally and in universities. It promotes the education, training and practice of engineering among women, provides a forum for the exchange of opinions and experience and provides networking opportunities. It also has links with other women's organisations and represents women engineers with government and policy-making institutions.

C. GOVERNMENT/OFFICIAL AGENCIES

Advice, Conciliation and Arbitration Service (Acas)
Head Office
Brandon House
180 Borough High Street
London SE1 1LW
national helpline 08457 47 47 47 (Monday to Friday 9.00–16.30)
www.acas.org.uk
Acas offers a whole spectrum of services ranging from helping with dispute resolution and individual problems to running interactive seminars and fine-tuning HR systems for the future. Its national helpline answers over 750,000 calls a year, giving confidential advice on employment matters and Acas delivers around 500 seminars

providing practical help. Acas publications provide advice and guidance on best practice in the workplace. Publications can be ordered by calling 0870 242 9090 or by visiting the website.

Age Positive
Age Positive Team
Dept for Work & Pensions
Room W8d
Moorfoot
Sheffield S1 4PQ
e-mail *agepositive@dwp.gsi.gov.uk*
www.agepositive.gov.uk
The government campaign promoting age diversity in employment, increasing the retention of people over 50 in work and encouraging employers to use age-diverse practices. The website includes current news on age diversity, details of events, consultation, legislation and statistics on older workers. The campaign also publishes a code of practice.

Commission for Racial Equality
St Dunstan's House
201–211 Borough High Street
London SE1 1GZ
tel 020 7939 0000
fax 020 7939 0001
e-mail *info@cre.gov.uk*
www.cre.gov.uk
Publicly funded, non-governmental body set up under the Race Relations Act 1976 to tackle racial discrimination and promote racial equality. It works in both the public and private sectors to encourage fair treatment and promote equal opportunities, and runs campaigns to raise awareness of race issues.

Criminal Records Bureau
PO Box 110
Liverpool L3 6ZZ
info line 0870 90 90 811
registration application line 0870 90 90 822

disclosure application line 0870 90 90 844
minicom 0870 90 90 344
www.crb.gov.uk; *www.disclosure.gov.uk*
An executive agency of the Home Office. Its disclosure service for England and Wales gives access to records held by the police, Department of Health and the Department for Education and Skills. The service helps recruiting agencies and organisations to make more thorough recruitment checks, especially for jobs involving regular contact with children and vulnerable adults. There is a fee for this service; however, standard and enhanced disclosures for volunteers in sensitive positions will be issued free of charge. Applications are made via a registered body.

Equal Opportunities Commission (EOC)
Arndale House
Arndale Centre
Manchester M4 3EQ
tel 0845 601 5901
fax 0161 838 1733
e-mail *info@eoc.org.uk*
www.eoc.org.uk

In Scotland: St Stephen's House
279 Bath Street
Glasgow G2 4JL
tel 0845 601 5901
fax 0141 248 5834
e-mail *scotland@eoc.org.uk*

In Wales: Windsor House
Windsor Lane
Cardiff CF10 3GE
tel 029 2034 3552
fax 029 2064 1079
e-mail *wales@eoc.org.uk*

EOC media enquiries:
36 Broadway
London SW1H 0BH
tel 020 7222 0004
fax 020 7222 2810
e-mail *media@eoc.org.uk*
Established under the Sex Discrimination Act in 1975 as an
independent statutory body with the following powers: to work
towards the elimination of discrimination on the grounds of sex or
marriage; to promote equality of opportunity for women and men; to
keep under review the Sex Discrimination Act and the Equal Pay Act;
and to provide legal advice and assistance to individuals who have
been discriminated against.

European Women's Lobby (EWL/LEF)
18 Rue Hydraulique
B-1210 Bruxelles
tel +32.2.217.90.20
fax +32.2.219.84.51
e-mail *ewl@womenlobby.org*
www.womenlobby.org
Lobbying organisation.

Public Appointments Unit (PAU)
Cabinet Office
Admiralty Arch
The Mall
London SW1A 2WH
tel 020 7276 2483
minicom 020 7276 2482
fax 020 7276 2488
e-mail *public.appointments.unit@cabinet-office.x.gsi.gov.uk*
www.publicappointments.gov.uk
www.publicappts-vacs.gov.uk (public appointments vacancies)
There are over 800 public bodies sponsored by UK government
departments, from the Adult Learning Inspectorate to the British
Waterways Board. Public appointees sit on the boards of these
organisations. They are involved in decisions that develop, shape or

deliver government policy and public services – decisions that affect everyone's life. To see details of current public appointments vacancies, visit the website.

Women and Equality Unit (WEU)
35 Great Smith Street
London SW1P 3BQ
tel 0845 001 0029
e-mail *info-womenandequalityunit@dti.gsi.gov.uk*
www.womenandequalityunit.gov.uk
The Government believes in a modern Britain that fosters and uses the talents of all groups; that promotes opportunity for everyone; and that views diversity as a source of competitive advantage and higher productivity. The Ministers for Women, supported by the Women and Equality Unit (WEU) are responsible for promoting and realising the benefits of diversity in the economy and more widely. They develop policies relating to gender equality and ensure that work on equality across government as a whole is co-ordinated.

Women's National Commission (WNC)
Department of Trade and Industry
35 Great Smith Street
London SW1P 3BQ
tel 020 7276 2553
fax 020 7276 2563
e-mail *wnc@dti.gsi.gov.uk*
www.thewnc.org.uk
The umbrella body of 240 UK women's organisations and the official independent advisory body, giving the views of women to government. It liaises with and is consulted by the Women and Equality Unit (see below) as well as other government departments. The WNC is concerned with all aspects of life that affect women and operates through consulting its membership, conferences and seminars on specific topics, working groups, lobbying, newsletters and open public meetings.

D. CHARITABLE/VOLUNTARY ORGANISATIONS

Charity People
38 Bedford Place
London WC1B 5JH
tel 020 7299 8700
www.charitypeople.com
The leading recruitment consultancy dedicated to the non-profit sector. Its consultants are specialists in recruiting staff of all functions, at all levels, for organisations across the entire not-for-profit sector, including charities, housing associations, NGOs, arts and the public sector. It also has a senior appointments division, and a weekly online jobs bulletin on its website.

Citizens Advice (CAB)
Myddelton House
115–123 Pentonville Road
London N1 9LZ
tel 020 7833 2181
fax 020 7833 4371
www.citizensadvice.org.uk
The Citizens Advice service helps people resolve their money, legal and other problems by providing information and advice, and by influencing policymakers. The address and phone number of the local CAB can be found in the telephone directory and on the website. For online information visit *www.adviceguide.org.uk* which gives basic advice and information on your rights in all areas including housing, debt, benefits, consumer rights and family matters. To enquire about local volunteering opportunities call 08451 264 263 (local rate).

Dress for Success London
Unit 2, 83–93 Shepperton Road
London N1 3DF
tel 020 7288 1770
fax 020 7288 1761
e-mail *London@dressforsuccess.org*
www.dressforsuccess.org
An international charity based in London providing interview-

appropriate clothing to low-income women, making tailored transitions into the workforce. Clients must be referred through member organisations, e.g. Training for Life, Newtec, Camden Itech, Getting London Working. Full list available from Dress for Success.

National Association of Councils for Voluntary Service
177 Arundel Street
Sheffield S1 2NU
tel 0114 278 6636
fax 0114 278 7004
e-mail *nacvs@nacvs.org.uk*
www.nacvs.org.uk
Founded in 1991, the National Association of Councils for Voluntary Service has more than 300 CVS members in both cities and rural areas. They promote effective local voluntary and community action by providing member CVS with a range of support services.

National Council for Voluntary Organisations (NCVO)
helpdesk tel 0800 2798 798
www.ncvo-vol.org.uk
The umbrella body for the voluntary sector in England as the 'voice of the voluntary sector'. With a growing membership of over 3,300 voluntary organisations, NCVO represents the sector to policy makers and government, and campaigns on issues affecting the sector. Services include a freephone helpdesk, a free online 'knowledgebase' at *www.askncvo.org.uk*, policy briefings, information networks, events and publications.

National Women's Register (NWR)
3a Vulcan House
Vulcan Road North
Norwich NR6 6AQ
tel 01603 406767; 0845 4500 287
fax 01603 407003
e-mail *office@nwr.org*
www.nwr.org
NWR is for making friends locally, exploring new interests and meeting different women. It is a countrywide network of informal

groups that meet in each other's homes where lively-minded members exchange ideas, enjoy challenging discussions and share social events such as conferences and workshops.

One Parent Families (OPF)

255 Kentish Town Road
London NW5 2LX
lone parent helpline 0800 018 5026 (advice on maintenance and benefits available Monday to Friday, 9.00–17.00)
tel 020 7428 5400
fax 020 7482 4851
e-mail *susan@oneparentfamilies.org.uk*
www.oneparentfamilies.org.uk
Promotes the welfare of lone parents and their children and aims to overcome poverty, isolation and social exclusion. Offers parents the means to help themselves and their families by providing information and advice, working with communities and developing new solutions to meet changing needs. OPF provides a range of resources and information, and training and consultancy services for organisations and groups. Campaigns for national strategies to help lone parents who want to move from benefits to work, for improved access to education and training, and better recognition of the value of parenting.

Working for a Charity

The Peel Centre
Percy Circus
London WC1X 9EY
tel 020 7833 8220
fax 020 7833 1820
e-mail *enquiries@wfac.org.uk*
www.wfac.org
Exists to promote the voluntary sector as a positive career option for those seeking paid employment, and the opportunities and benefits of becoming a volunteer to people wanting unpaid work. Holds material about training, information and links to other websites and about working placements for hosting organisations.

E. SELF-EMPLOYMENT AND BUSINESS

Advice, Conciliation and Arbitration Service (Acas)
Head Office
Brandon House
180 Borough High Street
London SE1 1LW
national helpline 08457 47 47 47 (Monday to Friday 9.00–16.30)
www.acas.org.uk
Acas offers a whole spectrum of services ranging from helping with dispute resolution and individual problems to running interactive seminars and fine-tuning HR systems for the future. Its national helpline answers over 750,000 calls a year, giving confidential advice on employment matters and Acas delivers around 500 seminars providing practical help. Acas publications provide advice and guidance on best practice in the workplace. Publications can be ordered by calling 0870 242 9090 or by visiting the website.

Aurora Gender Capital Management
Albert Buildings
49 Queen Victoria Street
London EC4N 4SA
tel 020 7653 1909
fax 0709 228 7944
e-mail *admin@auroravoice.com*
www.network.auroravoice.com
Networking organisation for women-owned businesses. Aurora works to support women's individual business and career needs and also works at industry level to help companies throughout Europe to attract, retain, develop and advance women staff.

Black Women Mean Business (BWMB)
PO Box 11371
Stoke Newington
London N16 8TY
tel 020 7219 4426
e-mail *carbye@parliament.uk*
An initiative launched by Diane Abbott MP in 1993. She started the

organisation as a way of helping black women business owners to develop the skills and expertise needed to become successful entrepreneurs. Initially BWMB consisted of professionals based within her constituency in Hackney, but now it has members from across London and from other parts of the UK. It is a non-profit-making organisation. Each year it hosts an annual reception for members as well as smaller workshops, seminars and specific one-off events, all with the aim of encouraging networking, sharing information and enhancing business acumen.

British Association of Women Entrepreneurs (BAWE)
Suite F, 123–125 Gloucester Place
London W1H 3DB
tel 020 7935 0085
fax 020 7224 0582
e-mail *woutersz@aol.com*
www.bawe-uk.uk.org
Non-profit professional organisation founded in 1954 and affiliated to Les Femmes Chefs d'Entreprises Mondiales (FCEM). Aims to encourage personal development of members and provides opportunities for them to grow their businesses through networking, the BAWE website focuses on marketing and advertising, conferences and trade missions. Also provides mentoring and training.

British Franchise Association
Thames View
Newtown Road
Henley on Thames RG9 1HG
tel 01491 578050
fax 01491 573517
e-mail *mailroom@british-franchise.org.uk*
www.british-franchise.org.uk
Regulatory and non-profit-making body responsible for developing and promoting fair and ethical franchising through its member companies. Publishes a code of conduct and annual survey and directory of members.

Business in the Community (BITC)
137 Shepherdess Walk
London N1 7RQ
tel 0870 600 2482
e-mail *information@bitc.org.uk*
www.bitc.org.uk
Members of BITC are committed to continually improving their positive impact on society. It has a core membership of 700 companies. (See also Opportunity Now, page 196.)

Business Link
tel advice line 0845 600 9006
www.businesslink.org
A national business-advice service, backed by the Department of Trade & Industry, which exists to provide businesses with quick and easy access to the advice, information and support they need to help them achieve their goals.

Chambers of Commerce
Many chambers of commerce have groups for businesswomen. To find details of local chambers, consult the local classified business telephone directory under 'Chambers of Commerce' or check the website: *www.chamberonline.co.uk.*

Chartered Management Institute
Management House
Cottingham Road
Corby
Northants NN17 1TT
tel 01536 204222
fax 01536 401013
e-mail *mic.enquiries@managers.org.uk*
www.managers.org.uk
Formed in 1992 from the merger of the British Institute of Management and the Institution of Industrial Managers and became the Chartered Management Institute in 2002. It is the UK's leading organisation for professional management, with members, both individual and corporate, from all sectors, both public and private. It offers members

access to and advice on management training and development programmes, courses, CV and career factsheets, networking opportunities
and a range of professional journals and publications.

City Women's Network
Administrative Office
PO Box 353
Uxbridge UB10 0UN
tel 01895 272 178
e-mail *cwn@byword.org*
www.citywomen.org
Network for senior executive women in and around London.
Members are professional women and business owners. Frequent
meetings and workshops are held.

Cranfield Centre for Developing Women Business Leaders
Cranfield School of Management
Cranfield University
Bedford
MK43 0AL
tel 01234 751 122
e-mail *v.singh@cranfield.ac.uk*
www.cranfield.ac.uk/som/ccdwbl
Researches the kinds of organisations that women entrepreneurs set
up, and the leadership models they use. Of particular interest are
women who left corporate life to start their own businesses.

European Federation of Black Women Business Owners
2 Tunstall Road
London SW9 8DA
tel 020 7978 9488
fax 020 7987 9490
e-mail *yvonne.thompson@asapcomms.co.uk*
www.efbwbo.net
Launched in October 1996 and now has more than 4,000 members in
the UK, France, Belgium and Holland. Holds an annual conference
with workshops and makes awards as well as providing networking
opportunities and support for minority businesses.

Federation of Small Businesses
Sir Frank Whittle Way
Blackpool Business Park
Blackpool
Lancs FY4 2FE
UK press office: 2 Catherine Place
London SW1E 6HE
tel 01253 336300
fax 01253 348046
e-mail *ho@fsb.org.uk*
www.fsb.org.uk
The voice of the small business sector with 182,000 members. Non-party-political campaigning pressure group with regional offices, promoting the interests of small business owners and managers. Issues a bi-monthly magazine.

High Street Banks
All the high street banks provide advice and support to those wishing to start up and run a small business. Help ranges from CD-roms to special business accounts, software, guides and business support helplines. All give advice on preparing a business plan and where to find possible sources of finance.

Homeworking.com
c/o Knowledge Computing
9 Ashdown Drive
Borehamwood
Herts WD6 4LZ
fax 0870 284 8769
e-mail *admin@homeworking.org*
www.homeworking.com
Site was established in 1999 for those wanting to get started, or already working from home. Runs a forum for support, and provides information on what is entailed in working at home, whether it is suitable for you and some of the practical advice needed for the self-employed. Includes case studies, advice on how to check out offers, debt advice and IT support.

Industrial Society, *see* The Work Foundation, page 199.

National Unit for Women's Enterprise
Scottish Enterprise
Small Business Services
150 Broomielaw
Atlantic Quay
Glasgow G2 8LU
tel 0141 248 2700
fax 0141 221 3217
e-mail *enquiries@scotent.co.uk*
www.scottishbusinesswomen.com
Targeted at women considering or in process of starting a business and
women running companies. This is a business support service offering
advice, mentors, skills training, etc. and the website is part of the
Women into Business Programme run by the Scottish Enterprise
Network and partners.

New Ways to Work, *see* Working Families, page 200.

Opportunity Now
137 Shepherdess Walk
London N1 7RQ
tel 020 7566 8714
fax 020 7253 1877
www.bitc.org.uk
Previously known as Opportunity 2000 (launched in 1991 by Business
in the Community), and relaunched in summer 1999, Opportunity
Now works with employers to realise the potential and business
benefits that women at every level contribute to the workforce. It now
has 360 participating employer members drawn from a wide range of
organisations in the public, private and education sectors.

Prowess
Lion House
20–28 Muspole Street
Norwich NR3 1DJ
tel 01603 762 355

fax 01603 227 090
e-mail *admin@prowess.org.uk*
www.prowess.org.uk
Trade association for organisations committed to providing women-friendly business support. The Prowess website has map-based links to local women-friendly business support providers across the UK and also inspirational stories of ordinary women who have started their own businesses.

Swiftwork
PO Box 120
Tunbridge Wells
TN5 7ZA
tel 01580 201 661
fax 01580 201 660
e-mail *enquiries@swiftwork.com*
contact Gill Hayward
www.swiftwork.com
Specialises in flexible working and work-life balance, helping organisations to capitalise on the challenges of new ways of working in the 21st century. Swiftwork provides a free membership forum for work returners, homeworkers and all people who are working, or want to work, flexibly. This includes online help and advice and a freelance directory for people who are available to work flexibly or part-time.

UK Online for Business
tel 0845 715 2000
www.ukonlineforbusiness.gov.uk
A DTI-led partnership between industry and government that helps UK businesses both understand and realise the substantial competitive benefits of using information and communications technologies (ICTs) across the whole of the organisation. Provides information and advice through a network of advisers based in Business Links in England and their counterparts in Scotland, Wales and Northern Ireland, an extensive network of partners from the ICT, business and public sectors, a range of innovative and effective publications and business tools available free online and offline, and a programme of events.

Women's Employment, Enterprise and Training Unit (WEETU)
Sackville Place
44–48 Magdalen Street
Norwich NR3 1JU
tel 01603 767 367
fax 01603 666 693
e-mail *outreach@weetu.org*
www.weetu.org
Not-for-profit organisation for women in the Norfolk and Waveney area that delivers a range of practical services to help improve their economic situation. Provides information, advice, support and a range of training courses to help women gain access to learning, employment and self-employment opportunities. All the services are free and assistance is provided towards the cost of travel and childcare expenses.

Women at Work
e-mail *info@womenatwork.co.uk*
www.womenatwork.co.uk
Membership organisation that consists of an online UK directory and database of women in business, including women running small businesses, the self-employed, sole traders and freelancers.

Women In Business for Merseyside
e-mail *ellen.kerr@womeninbusiness.co.uk*
www.womeninbusiness.co.uk
Network that brings together and supports women in business, management, the professions and education and facilitates networking opportunities. Also provides business-relevant workshops. Launched in 1994 for women in the north-west.

Women in Docklands
Chair: Heather Waring
tel 020 8220 6919
e-mail *heather@waringwell.com*
Non-profit organisation set up in 1991 as a network for business women working or living in Docklands in East London. It welcomes business women from all areas of the capital and beyond, who wish

to expand their contacts in the region. Members range from sole traders to women in senior-level corporate posts, from the public, private and voluntary sectors.

Women into the Network
Durham Business School
University of Durham
Mill Hill Lane
Durham DH1 3LB
tel 0191 334 5502
fax 0191 334 5499
e-mail *info@networkingwomen.co.uk*
www.networkingwomen.co.uk
Networking initiative that aims to integrate women entrepreneurs into existing business networks in the north-east of England and nationally. It also works to bridge the gap between providers of business and professional support.

The Work Foundation
Peter Runge House
3 Carlton House Terrace
London SW1Y 5DG
tel 0870 165 6700
fax 0870 165 6701
e-mail *contactcentre@theworkfoundation.com*
www.theworkfoundation.com
Formerly the Industrial Society, an independent not-for-profit think-tank and consultancy with a large membership base. Conducts research, campaigning and practical interventions with the aim of improving productivity and quality of working life in the UK. Runs the Employers for Work-Life Balance website, which has practical advice, case studies and information on work-life issues for employers and policy-makers.

Working Families
1–3 Berry Street
London EC1V 0AA
tel 020 7253 7243
e-mail *office@workingfamilies.co.uk*
www.workingfamilies.org.uk
Formed in November 2003 when Parents at Work and New Ways to Work amalgamated under their new name. It is a campaigning charity that supports and gives a voice to working parents and carers, and helps employers create workplaces that encourage work-life balance. It holds best-practice seminars and training workshops around the country and runs the Employer of the Year Awards and the Best Boss competition. Free factsheets can be obtained by calling 020 7490 2414 and there is a freephone legal helpline on 0800 013 1313.

F. FINANCE AND LEGAL SERVICES

Association of Women Solicitors
The Law Society
114 Chancery Lane
London WC2A 1PL
tel 020 7320 5793
e-mail *enquiries@womensolicitors.org.uk*
www.lawsociety.org.uk
Works to promote the professional and business interests of women solicitors.

Career Development Loan (CDL)
tel 0800 585 505
www.lifelonglearning.co.uk
A deferred repayment bank loan to help pay for vocational learning or education. The DfES pays the interest on the loan while recipients are learning. It is available to anyone over the age of 18 who lives in Great Britain and intends to study and then work in the UK or EU. To find out more about the CDL, contact their freephone number, where an adviser can give more information.

Department for Work and Pensions
Public Enquiry Office
The Adelphi
Room 112, 1–11 John Adam Street
London WC2N 6HT
tel 020 7712 2171 (Monday to Friday, 9.00–17.00)
fax 020 7712 2386
www.dwp.gov.uk
Website has information on benefits and services A–Z, families and children, working age, pensions and retirement. Gives contact details for other relevant government agencies.

Financial Services Authority
25 The North Colonnade
Canary Wharf
London E14 5HS
tel 020 7066 1000
consumer helpline 0845 606 1234
fax 020 7066 9713
e-mail *consumerhelp@fsa.gov.uk*
www.fsa.gov.uk/consumerhelp
The consumer helpline can answer general queries about financial products and services, give information on authorised firms or advisers and help with complaints. Issues factsheets and booklets and lists other useful sources of information.

Fiona Price & Partners Ltd
29 Ely Place
London EC1N 6TD
tel 020 7611 4700
fax 020 7611 4701
e-mail *advice@fionaprice.co.uk*
www.fionaprice.co.uk
Financial advisers specialising in independent financial and tax advice for women. Range of services includes personal financial planning, financial services for companies, tax services, financial seminars.

Law Society
www.solicitors-online.com
Quick way to find a solicitor on the Internet and designed for anyone looking for legal help. Also useful for advice centres, and information services. Information is updated daily from Law Society records, free of charge to users and firms. Data can be accessed by name, geographical area, specialism, and languages spoken. Website links are also listed.

Legal Services Commission (LSC)
85 Gray's Inn Road
London WC1X 8TX
tel 020 7759 0000
directory line 0845 608 1122 (all calls charged at local rate)
leaflet line 0845 300 0343
minicom 0845 609 6677 (directory line)
www.legalservices.gov.uk; *www.justask.org.uk*
The LSC replaced the Legal Aid Board in April 2000. It is responsible for the development and administration of two schemes in England and Wales: the Community Legal Service, which from 1 April 2000 replaced the old civil legal-aid scheme, and the Criminal Defence Service, which from 2 April 2001 replaced the old system of criminal legal aid. Contact details of CLS and CDS solicitors and advice agencies are available from the directory line or JustAsk! website. Information leaflets on LSC-funded work and general legal information leaflets are available from the leaflet line or the websites.

Office for the Pensions Advisory Service
11 Belgrave Road
London SW1V 1RB
tel helpline 0845 601 2923
www.opas.org.uk
Independent non-profit organisation providing information and advice on state, company, stakeholder and personal pension schemes. Will also help with problems, complaints and disputes. The work is undertaken mainly by a network of volunteer pension professionals.

Pensions Info-Line
The Pension Service (part of Department for Work & Pensions)
order line tel 0845 7 31 32 33
helpline tel 0800 99 1234
www.pensionguide.gov.uk
Free guides can be downloaded and include one on pensions for
women and another on pensions for the self-employed. The helpline
acts as a signpost on where to go for benefit and pension queries.

Rights of Women
52–54 Featherstone Street
London EC1Y 8RT
tel 020 7490 2562; advice line 020 7251 6577 (Tuesday to Thursday,
14.00–16.00; Friday, 12.00–1400)
fax 020 7490 5377
e-mail *info@row.org.uk*
www.rightsofwomen.org.uk
Works to attain justice and equality by informing, educating and
empowering women on their legal rights. Advice line gives free legal
advice for and by women. Rights of Women provides downloadable
information sheets and training for organisations. There is also
information on current research projects.

Taxing Nannies
28 Minchenden Crescent
London N14 7EL
tel 020 8882 6847
fax 020 8886 1624
e-mail *post@taxingnannies.co.uk*
www.taxingnannies.co.uk
Specialist payroll service for employers of nannies and domestic staff.
It produces payslips, deals with tax calculations and all Inland
Revenue correspondence. It also advises on SSP/SMP and other payroll matters. It issues information sheets on employers' responsibilities
and nanny-share implications. Monthly subscription.

Women in Banking and Finance (WIBF)
43 Keswick Road
West Wickham
Kent BR4 9AS
tel 020 8777 6902
fax 020 8777 7064
e-mail *wibf_ann@btopenworld.com*
www.wibf.org.uk
Non-profit-making networking group founded in 1980 and sponsored by banks and city institutions. It aims to empower its members in the banking and finance industry to realise their full potential. WIBF provides a Personal Excellence Programme (incorporating personal development, mentoring and coaching, media and presentation skills and professional development), Networking Beyond Boundaries and a senior executive programme. An Awards for Achievement lunch, annual address and Speaker Series give access to leaders in the banking and finance industry. WIBF publishes a bimonthly newsletter and the above programmes are currently available in both London and Scotland.

G. CHILDCARE, CARERS AND DISABLED PEOPLE

Carers UK
20–25 Glasshouse Yard
London EC1A 4JT
tel 020 7490 8818
fax 020 7490 8824
carersline 0808 808 7777
e-mail *info@ukcarers.org*
www.carersonline.org.uk
In September 2001 Carers National Association became Carers UK, known in the nations as Carers Scotland, Carers Wales and Carers Northern Ireland. There is also an area office in Manchester for the north of England. Carers UK is a campaigning organisation that provides information and advice to both carers and professionals, and raises awareness of carers' needs. CarersLine is a free advice line for carers, staffed by welfare rights, community care and benefits experts.

Carers UK believes that carers should be encouraged to continue with paid work if they wish to and it offers companies advice and training on developing carer-friendly policies.

Carers Online
www.carersonline.org.uk
Branches of Carers UK (see above), providing carers and others with national and local information. Local information is provided on county sites by Devon, Surrey and West Sussex county councils, and national information is given by Carers UK.

ChildcareLink
tel 0800 0 96 02 96 (freephone)
www.childcarelink.gov.uk
Launched in England and Scotland in December 1999 by the Department for Education & Skills and the Scottish Executive, with the aim of helping people back into the workplace by removing barriers to finding childcare. The service consists of a website and a national information line, and is able to provide contact details of local Children's Information Services (CIS; see below).

Childcare Plus Ltd
Unit 11, 1st floor west
Universal House
88–94 Wentworth Street
London E1 7SA
tel 020 7247 6338
fax 020 7247 5425
e-mail *info@startingupchildcare.co.uk*
www.startingupchildcare.co.uk
Specialist daycare development consultancy supplying solutions for the creation and expansion of childcare facilities across public, private and voluntary sectors.

Children's Information Service (CIS)
Local authorities have a legal duty to establish and maintain a service providing information to the public relating to the provision of childcare and related services in their area – a Children's Information

Service or CIS. CISs hold details on all registered childcare and early education providers in their area and make this available to parents. They can assist parents in finding provision that best meets their needs, for example, by providing information on childcare close to their workplace. They can also provide advice on how to choose a childcare provider, the service offered by different types of childcare provider, and information on other types of family support such as financial assistance. In many cases, CISs can also provide information on wider parenting and family issues. Details of your local service can be found via the ChildcareLink website or phone line (see above).

Daycare Trust
21 St George's Road
London SE1 6ES
tel 020 7840 3350 (hotline Monday to Friday, 10.00–17.00)
fax 020 7840 3355
e-mail *info@daycaretrust.org.uk*
www.daycaretrust.org.uk
National childcare charity that promotes quality affordable childcare for all. Has a childcare hotline, providing free information and advice for parents.

Disability Alliance
Universal House
88–94 Wentworth Street
London E1 7SA
tel 020 7247 8776 (voice and minicom, 10.00–16.00); 020 7247 8763 (rights advice line, Monday and Wednesday, 14.00–16.00)
fax 020 7247 8765
e-mail *office.da@dial.pipex.com*
www.disabilityalliance.org
Disability Alliance's chief aim is to improve the living standards of disabled people by breaking the link between poverty and disability. It gives disabled people, their families, carers and professional advisers information about social security benefit and other entitlements. It does this through the provision of advice, information, campaigning, research and training so that disabled people are fully aware of and able to claim their benefits. A 'headline' publication is

its annual *Disability Rights Handbook*, and, among other titles, the *Disability Rights Bulletin* is issued three times a year.

Early Years Online
e-mail *register@earlyyearsonline.co.uk*
www.earlyyearsonline.co.uk
Internet-based communication organisation focused on childcare provision and information. The site aims to provide a comprehensive directory of validated childcare provision nationally, to include after-school and holiday clubs, playgroups, childminder networks, crèches and nurseries, etc.

Gingerbread
7 Sovereign Court
Sovereign Close
London E1W 3HW
tel 020 7488 9300
fax 020 7488 9333
advice line 0800 018 4318 (Monday to Friday, 9.00–17.00)
e-mail *office@gingerbread.co.uk*
www.gingerbread.org.uk
Started in 1970, Gingerbread is a registered charity maintained by lone parents, with London and regional offices. It offers practical and emotional support to lone parents and speaks out for them in the media and politics. Gingerbread has an advice line, support groups, an e-mail discussion list, and training and consultancy packages suitable for employers, colleges, community organisations and local self-help groups.

Kids' Clubs Network
Bellerive House
3 Muirfield Crescent
London E14 9SZ
tel 020 7512 2112
info-line 020 7512 2100
fax 020 7512 2010
e-mail *information.office@kidsclubs.org.uk*
www.kidsclubs.org.uk

National charity developed to provide an information resource for both parents and the childcare sector. The website offers a comprehensive news information service providing updates on developments in childcare and government announcements; all Kids' Clubs Network's press releases and news briefings can be accessed. Kids' Clubs open before and after school and during the holidays and give children from four to fourteen a safe place to play. The network provides training, a quality-assurance programme and support and issues a bi-monthly magazine, a newsletter and other publications.

Maternity Alliance

Third floor west
2–6 Northburgh Street
London EC1V 0AY
tel 020 7490 7639
information line 020 7490 7638
fax 020 7014 1350
e-mail *info@maternityalliance.org.uk*
www.maternityalliance.org.uk
Advisers are available at certain times and the 24-hour recorded information line offers advice on antenatal care and health and safety at work, maternity leave and pay, returning to work, parental leave and time off for dependents. Gives details of changes in maternity leave and pay.

Mother@Work

www.motheratwork.co.uk
Launched autumn 2003, this is a total resource site for women who combine work, children and a personal life. It aims to discuss issues relevant to working mothers, from finance and childcare to legal and personal, health and shopping, alongside feature interviews with high-profile working mothers, and tips on making time stretch and also finding time for you.

Mumsnet

e-mail *contactus@mumsnet.com*
www.mumsnet.com
Set up by parents for parents to pool information, advice and

encouragement and discuss problems. Their first book, *Mums on Babies*, a unique guide to the first year, based on the practical experience of members, was published by Cassell Illustrated in 2003. *Mums on Pregnancy* is due out in January 2004.

National Childminding Association (NCMA)
8 Masons Hill
Bromley
Kent BR2 9EY
freephone information line 0800 169 4486
Ofsted helpline 0845 601 4771
www.ncma.org.uk
Promotes quality registered childminding in England and Wales. It aims to ensure that every registered childminder has access to services, training, information and support to do a professional job.

National Day Nurseries Association
Oak House
Woodvale Road
Brighouse
West Yorkshire HD6 4AB
tel 0870 7744 244
fax 0870 7744 243
e-mail *info@ndna.org.uk*
www.ndna.org.uk
National childcare charity that promotes quality childcare and education in the early years. Advises central and local government and the media on care and education in day nurseries. It offers training and quality assurance for daycare settings and information and guidance for parents.

Netmums
e-mail *enquiries@netmums.com*
www.netmums.com
Local information sites run by mums for mums to provide information and support for other local parents.

Parents at Work, *see* Working Families, page 211.

Pre-School Learning Alliance
69 Kings Cross Road
London WC1X 9LL
tel 020 7833 0991
e-mail *pla@pre-school.org.uk*
www.pre-school.org.uk
Represents and supports 16,000 community pre-schools in England.
Began in 1961 when self-help nursery schools were started by parents
in the absence of state provision.

Princess Royal Trust for Carers
142 The Minories
London EC3N 1LB
tel 020 7480 7788
fax 020 7481 4729
e-mail *info@carers.org*
www.carers.org.uk

In Scotland:
Campbell House
215 West Campbell Street
Glasgow G2 4TT
tel 0141 251 5066
fax 0141 224 4623
e-mail *infoScotland@carers.org*
National charity established in 1991. Provides information, support
and practical help for carers and has a national network of more than
a hundred independently managed carers centres across the UK. The
trust gives training and support for carers centres and raises funds for
development.

Royal Association for Disability and Rehabilitation (RADAR)
12 City Forum
250 City Road
London EC1V 8AF
tel 020 7250 3222

fax 020 7250 0212
e-mail *radar@radar.org.uk*
www.radar.org.uk
Established in 1977, RADAR is an umbrella organisation with nearly 700 member organisations of or for disabled people. It campaigns for the social inclusion of disabled people and supports campaigning organisations with tools and services to organisations of and for disabled people. Its work covers issues such as education, employment, social security, mobility and housing.

Taxing Nannies
28 Minchenden Crescent
London N14 7EL
tel 020 8882 6847
fax 020 8886 1624
e-mail *post@taxingnannies.co.uk*
www.taxingnannies.co.uk
Specialist payroll service for employers of nannies and domestic staff. It produces payslips, deals with tax calculations and all Inland Revenue correspondence. It also advises on SSP/SMP and other payroll matters. It issues information sheets on employers' responsibilities and nanny-share implications. Monthly subscription.

Working Families
1–3 Berry Street
London EC1V 0AA
tel 020 7253 7243
e-mail *office@workingfamilies.co.uk*
www.workingfamilies.org.uk
Formed in November 2003 when Parents at Work and New Ways to Work amalgamated under their new name. It is a campaigning charity that supports and gives a voice to working parents and carers, and helps employers create workplaces that encourage work-life balance. It holds best-practice seminars and training workshops around the country and runs the Employer of the Year Awards and the Best Boss competition. Free factsheets can be obtained by calling 020 7490 2414 and there is a freephone legal helpline on 0800 013 1313.

H. TRAINING AND SELF-DEVELOPMENT

There is a myriad of websites dealing with career advice and self-development. A small selection is given here, as well as listings of other training organisations.

ActiveSkills
e-mail *info@activeskills.com*
www.activeskills.com
Online training courses designed for individuals and companies who need to broaden their business skills. Courses are presented in short modules and priced in credits which may be purchased online, by cheque or by subscription. Courses are listed in a course directory.

Association for Coaching
66 Church Road
London W7 1LB
tel 020 8566 2400
e-mail *enquiries@associationforcoaching.com*
www.associationforcoaching.com
An independent non-profit professional body for coaches or organisations involved in coaching to develop, expand and achieve their goals. The aim is to promote best practice and raise the awareness and standards across the coaching and mentoring industry, while providing value-added benefits to its members.

C2 – The Graduate Career Shop
49–51 Gordon Square
London WC1H 0PN
tel 020 7554 4555
fax 020 7383 5876
e-mail *careershop@careers.lon.ac.uk*
www.careershop.co.uk
Provides information on careers, personal consultations, psychometrics, etc. C2 works with graduates (or broadly equivalent level), career changers and re-entrants. It offers brief and long one-to-one guidance as well as online assistance for those who cannot easily get into central London. C2 works with clients from around the world.

There is a charge for advice sessions and Career Change evening seminars. Open Monday, Tuesday and Thursday, 9.30–17.00 and by appointment from 17.00–20.00; Wednesday, 9.30–20.00, and Friday, 11.00–17.00.

Changing Direction
PO Box 164
Pinner
Middlesex HA5 3YL
tel 020 8868 7818
e-mail *dianawolfin@changingdirection.com*
www.changingdirection.com
Provides training, workshops and consultations for groups and individuals on all aspects of the return-to-work process, as well as coping strategies for work-life balance.

Chartered Management Institute
Management House
Cottingham Road
Corby
Northants NN17 1TT
tel 01536 204222
fax 01536 401013
e-mail *enquiries@managers.org.uk*
www.managers.org.uk
Formed in 1992 from the merger of the British Institute of Management and the Institution of Industrial Managers and became the Chartered Management Institute in 2002. It is the UK's leading organisation for professional management, with members, both individual and corporate, from all sectors, both public and private. It offers members access to and advice on management training and development programmes, courses, CV and career factsheets, networking opportunities and a range of professional journals and publications.

Chartered Institute of Personnel & Development (CIPD)
CIPD House
Camp Road
Wimbledon SW19 4UX

tel 020 8263 3311
fax 020 8263 3250
e-mail *careers@cipd.co.uk*
www.cipd.co.uk
The IPD (now CIPD) was formed by the amalgamation some years ago of the Institute of Personnel Management and Institute of Training & Development. It received chartered status in 2000, and is a centre of excellence in setting standards in management and development of people. It is the largest single organisation in Europe representing professionals working in people management and has a membership of more than 118,000. The CIPD website provides an information service on employment law and bills in progress, and there is also a legal advisory service.

Coaching and Mentoring Network
41–43 Oxford Road
Oxford OX4 4PF
tel 0870 733 3313
fax 0870 733 3314
e-mail *annabg@coachingnetwork.org.uk*
www.coachingnetwork.org.uk
Leading free and independent information and networking resource dedicated to coaching and mentoring. Provides help for both those interested in using and providing coaching and mentoring services. Includes articles, bookshop, news and events, online discussion forum and links to other useful services.

Cranfield Centre for Developing Women Business Leaders
Cranfield School of Management
Cranfield University
Bedford
MK43 0AL
tel 01234 751 122
e-mail *v.singh@cranfield.ac.uk*
www.cranfield.ac.uk/som/ccdwbl
Researches the kinds of organisations that women entrepreneurs set up, and the leadership models they use. Of particular interest are women who left corporate life to start their own businesses.

Daphne Jackson Trust
Trust Director: Jenny Woolley
Fellowship Administrator: Sue Smith
tel 01483 689 166
e-mail *djmft@surrey.ac.uk*
www.daphnejackson.org
Charitable organisation that helps women and men retrain and return
to science, engineering and technology careers in both academia and
industry, after a break due to family commitments. Two-year part-time
paid fellowships are awarded, during which the fellows are able to
work on a research project, retrain and learn new skills to enable them
to find work. The trust runs the country's foremost returner's scheme
and has awarded over 100 fellowships with a 98-per-cent success rate
for returning scientists.

Farnham Castle International Briefing and Conference Centre
Farnham Castle
Farnham
Surrey GU9 0AG
tel 01252 721194
fax 01252 719277
e-mail *info@farnhamcastle.com*
www.farnhamcastle.com
Leading provider of intercultural briefing and training, which helps
individuals, partners and their families to prepare to live and work
effectively anywhere in the world. Using a large database of experts,
Farnham provides a flexible and wide range of programmes, including
country and business briefings for any country in the world,
repatriation, workshops on general intercultural awareness as well as
working effectively with specific cultures or nationalities, cross-
cultural communication, presentation and negotiation skills training,
plus language tuition.

Focus Information Services
13 Prince of Wales Terrace
London W8 5PG
tel 020 7937 7799
helpline 020 7937 0050 (Monday to Thursday, 10.00–14.00)

fax 020 7937 9482
e-mail *office@focus-info.org*
www.focus-info.org
A non-profit organisation that supports international assignees and
their families in the UK. Established in 1982, Focus provides
information and networking opportunities for its members, enabling
them to integrate rapidly into their new environment. Among several
services, Focus provides a career development programme to its
members. This programme offers career assistance to accompanying
partners in assignments in the UK, by teaching the basics of effective
job searching and encouraging them to work in small groups.

Graduate Prospects
Prospects House
Booth Street East
Manchester M13 9EP
www.prospects.ac.uk
The UK's official graduate careers website which has a section on
mature students, accessible via the 'Your Background Issues' link.

Hillcroft College
South Bank
Surbiton
Surrey KT6 6DF
tel 020 8399 2688
fax 020 8390 9171
e-mail *enquiry@hillcroft.ac.uk*
www.hillcroft.ac.uk
The only publicly funded adult residential college for women in the
UK. Aims to help women achieve their full potential by progressing to
higher education, vocational training or employment. Programmes
cover a wide range of subjects and for many no formal qualifications
are needed. Some adult bursaries are available to give students
financial support. Women can attend either full-time or part-time and
many courses are run over a series of weekends. Staff at the college
are expert at helping returners adapt to an academic environment.

Institute of Career Guidance (ICG)
Third floor, Copthall House
1 New Road
Stourbridge
West Midlands DY8 1PH
tel 01384 376464
fax 01384 440830
e-mail *hq@icg-uk.org*
www.icg-uk.org
Since 1922 ICG has been the largest professional organisation for careers guidance professionals. It represents the views of its members to Westminster, Whitehall and the media, and provides training and development opportunities for guidance professionals.

The Institute of Leadership & Management
1 Giltspur Street
London EC1A 9DD
tel 020 7294 2470; 020 7294 3053 (for nearest centre)
fax 020 7294 2402
e-mail: *marketing@i-l-m.com*
www.nebsmgt.co.uk
The awarding body for general and specialist management qualifications. Group workshops and programmes tailored to the individual using self-study materials are run at accredited centres. Programmes are available in the UK and Ireland, also in Europe, the Middle East, Southern Africa, Asia, South America and the West Indies. There are 1,300 accredited centres.

Institute of Training and Occupational Learning (ITOL)
PO Box 69
Hazel Grove
Stockport SK7 4FR
tel 0161 483 4577
fax 0161 484 0576
e-mail *admin@itol.co.uk*
www.traininginstitute.co.uk
Promotes the development and professional standing of those in the fields of training, assessment and vocational education. It was

launched in February 2000. ITOL sponsors research and issues a bi-annual journal. The website allows the opportunity to contact other members and network via the electronic bulletin board. Continuous professional development is encouraged and is mandatory for Fellows and Members.

Learndirect
tel 0800 101 901 (helpline)
www.learndirect.co.uk
Learndirect has created a suite of courses which allow people and businesses to learn in 'bite-size chunks'. Available online, users can work at their own pace and at times that suit them, wherever they have access to the Internet – at Learndirect learning centres, at home or at work. The courses cover IT skills; business skills; the basics of reading, writing and numbers; retail and distribution; multimedia; environmental services; and automotive components.

Learndirect National Learning Advice Line
helpline 0800 100 900
www.learndirect-advice.co.uk
Gives impartial information about learning and helps people decide what, where and how they want to learn. The online database of courses that supports the helpline holds details of more than half a million courses from providers nationwide, as well as Learndirect's own courses.

Learning and Skills Council
Cheylesmore House
Quinton Road
Coventry CV1 2WT
tel 0845 019 4170
helpline 0870 900 6800
e-mail *info@lsc.gov.uk*
www.lsc.gov.uk
Responsible for funding and planning education and training for over-16-year-olds in England, other than in universities. It operates through 47 local offices and a national office in Coventry, and was set up in April 2001. Its work covers further education, work-based training and

young people, workforce development, adult and community learning and information, advice and guidance for adults, as well as education business links.

National Academic Recognition Information Centre for the UK (UK NARIC)
ECCTIS LTD
Oriel House
Oriel Road
Cheltenham
Glos GL50 1XP
tel 01242 260010
fax 01242 258611
e-mail *enquiries@ecctis.co.uk*
www.naric.org.uk
Run under contract to the Department for Education and Skills. It is a source for information and advice on the comparability of overseas qualifications with those from the UK. Also advises individuals and other organisations on registration with professional bodies and employment in the UK.

National Institute of Adult Continuing Education (NIACE)
20 Princess Road West
Leicester LE1 6TP
tel 0116 204 4200
fax 0116 285 4514
e-mail *enquiries@niace.org.uk*
www.niace.org.uk
Non-governmental organisation for adult learning in England and Wales. Website gives news, details of conferences and publications, campaigns and projects, and funding information.

National Mentoring Network
1st floor, Charles House
Albert Street
Eccles M30 0PW
tel 0161 787 8600
fax 0161 787 8100

e-mail *enquiries@nmn.org.uk*
www.nmn.org.uk
The network has 1,500 member organisations in the UK. It aims to promote the development of mentoring, offer advice and support to those wishing to set up or develop mentoring programmes, and provide a forum for the exchange of information and good practice. It was set up in 1994 and is funded by membership fees and support from business and government departments. Members include colleges, career services, businesses, voluntary groups and others. It publishes a Network Directory and other publications.

New Deal
tel 0845 606 2626 (daily 7.00–23.00); 0845 606 0680 (textphone)
www.newdeal.gov.uk
A government programme to support unemployed people and help them find work. It has programmes for those who are 25 plus, 50 plus, disabled people, lone parents, etc. Everyone on a programme gets a personal adviser for one-to-one advice, help with job-search skills, writing CVs and interview skills, plus other practical support.

The Open University (OU)
tel 01908 274066
www.open.ac.uk
The world's leading distance-education institution using 'supported open learning'. More than 2 million people have used the OU to enter into university study from their homes and workplaces - many of whom would not have gained access to conventional universities (the OU has no prerequisites for its undergraduate courses).

The Springboard Consultancy
Holwell
East Down
Barnstaple
Devon EX31 4NZ
tel 01271 850828
fax 01271 850130
e-mail *office@springboardconsultancy.com*
www.springboardconsultancy.com

Delivers a work and personal development programme spread over three months specifically for women. Programme comprises a workbook, four one-day workshops, role models, a flexible support system and networking skills.

Teacher Training Agency
Portland House
Stag Place
London SW1E 5TT
tel 020 7925 3700
e-mail *teaching@ttainfo.co.uk*
www.tta.gov.uk
National organisation that aims to raise standards in schools by improving the quality of teacher training, teaching and school leadership.

UK-HRD
www.ukhrd.com
A free-to-join e-mail-based discussion forum for training, human resource and people development specialists. It comprises a moderated daily discussion digest e-mailed directly to those registered, where people ask questions, share experiences and discuss issues affecting them in their working lives. Around 8,000 people have registered to receive and contribute to the UK-HRD digests, ranging from experienced trainers to those working on their own. A membership site (paid) offers further resources and benefits including the UK-HRD archive of all past discussion.

Women's Employment, Enterprise and Training Unit (WEETU)
Sackville Place
44–48 Magdalen Street
Norwich NR3 1JU
tel 01603 767 367
fax 01603 666 693
e-mail *outreach@weetu.org*
www.weetu.org
Not-for-profit organisation for women in the Norfolk and Waveney area that delivers a range of practical services to help improve their

economic situation. Provides information, advice, support and a range of training courses to help women gain access to learning, employment and self-employment opportunities. All the services are free and assistance is provided towards the cost of travel and childcare expenses.

Working for a Charity
The Peel Centre
Percy Circus
London WC1X 9EY
tel 020 7833 8220
fax 020 7833 1820
e-mail *enquiries@wfac.org.uk*
www.wfac.org
Exists to promote the voluntary sector as a positive career option for those seeking paid employment, and the opportunities and benefits of becoming a volunteer to people wanting unpaid work. Holds material about training, information and links to other websites and about working placements for hosting organisations.

Women's Education in Building (WEB)
12–14 Malton Road
London W10 5UP
tel 020 8968 9139
fax 020 8964 0255
e-mail *info@womenseducationinbuilding.org.uk*
www.womenseducationinbuilding.org.uk
Women's organisation that for 20 years has been working to promote training and careers for women in construction, focusing on manual trades. It offers a unique package of advice, support, free training leading to NVQ or equivalent qualifications, help with childcare and materials costs, positive role models and confidence-building, alongside work experience in the trades. It also runs general pre-vocational and return-to-study courses for women who are not yet ready for vocational training. WEB operates from three centres in London, including its new centre in Stratford which offers extensive support, premises and loans for new women-led small businesses as well as some help for men facing multiple barriers to work and education.

I. RECRUITMENT AGENCIES

Specialist recruitment agencies exist for specific professions – e.g. nursing, legal, accountancy – and some agencies focus particularly on office-based personnel or administrative staff. There are also agencies that recruit in the voluntary or charity sectors and others that specialise in interim management. Those that appear below are only a small selection and the list does not claim to be comprehensive.

Apex Charitable Trust
St Alphage House
Wingate Annexe
2 Fore Street
London EC2Y 5DA
Jobcheck telephone helpline 0870 608 4567 (Monday to Friday, 10.00–17.00)
fax 020 7638 5977
e-mail *jobcheck@apextrust.com*
www.apextrust.com
Founded in 1965, the trust promotes employment opportunities for ex-offenders by providing them with the skills needed in the labour market, and works with employers to break down the barriers to employment. The helpline provides information on ex-offender employment issues.

Charity People
38 Bedford Place
London WC1B 5JH
tel 020 7299 8700
www.charitypeople.com
The leading recruitment consultancy dedicated to the non-profit sector. Its consultants are specialists in recruiting staff of all functions, at all levels, for organisations across the entire not-for-profit sector, including charities, housing associations, NGOs, arts and the public sector. It also has a senior appointments division, and a weekly online jobs bulletin on its website.

Execs on the Net
tel 0870 727 0305
fax 0870 727 0325
e-mail *info@eotn.co.uk*
www.eotn.co.uk
Provides a selection of executive appointments, interim management appointments and consultancies across a range of industrial and commercial sectors. Also provides help on CV writing, interview techniques and psychometric assessment.

Fish4
www.fish4jobs.co.uk
The UK's most visited recruitment website advertising over 30,000 jobs by category, location and type, covering a variety of sectors and employers. It offer recruiter profiles, advice on interviews, legal rights, etc.

Forties People
11–13 Dowgate Hill
London EC4R 2ST
tel 020 7329 4044
fax 020 7329 4540
e-mail *info@fortiespeople.net*
www.fortiespeople.net
Recruitment consultancy for the over-forties. Committed to equal opportunities for all, with skills being the selection criterion.

Global Networker
e-mail *pat@global-networker.com*
www.global-networker.com
Offers two services to help spouses and partners of globally mobile employees to find work. Firstly, it runs networking events in London to help partners meet each other and potential employers, and to learn about networking and other job-search skills. Secondly, it runs a website with a range of useful reference information about job search in London, job search in other global capital cities, and general advice about portable careers. Global Networker can be contacted through its website.

Jobcentre Plus
Room 607, Caxton House
Tothill Street
London SW1H 9NA
tel 020 7273 6060; 020 7273 6222 (textphone)
fax 020 7273 6143
e-mail *leigh.lewis@jobcentreplus.gov.uk*
www.jobcentreplus.gov.uk (details of job vacancies, benefits and
Jobcentre Plus)
www.worktrain.gov.uk (details of job vacancies and learning
opportunities)
A service for people of working age. From April 2002 it replaced the
Employment Service, which ran jobcentres and parts of the Benefits
Agency that helped people of working age with benefits through social
security offices. Local jobcentres hold details of vacancies in the area
and nationally, and give information and advice about financial help
and childcare.

Local Authorities
Local authorities hold lists of council vacancies at all levels in the area
and can be accessed on the Internet, e.g. *www.barnet.gov.uk*.

Maturity Works
Airport House
Purley Way
Croydon CR0 0XZ
tel 020 8667 0175
fax 020 8667 0558
email *enquiries@maturityworks.co.uk*
www.maturityworks.co.uk
Aims to promote better recruitment practice by employers and give
the older worker access to the best opportunities available. As well as
more than 300 advertised vacancies targeting work returners, the
website also provides essential information and advice. It raises
awareness of how age discrimination works and how to combat it. It
also puts companies and older workers in touch with each other for
their mutual benefit.

Monster
e-mail *userservices@monster.co.uk*
www.monster.co.uk
'The world's leading career network' with job-search facilities for UK, European and global opportunities. Its career centre has articles on CV writing, interviews, job hunting, networking, career development, tax and pensions, and issues such as work and family, career change and retraining.

Reed, the recruitment group
www.reed.co.uk
More than 250 branches throughout the UK and Ireland, plus the recruitment website carries more than 100,000 opportunities from 39,000 recruiters. For nearest branch, see website or *Yellow Pages*. Free self-managed IT training available to candidates seeking work through the consultancy by arrangement with local branch.

Swiftwork
PO Box 120
Tunbridge Wells
TN5 7ZA
tel 01580 201 661
fax 01580 201 660
e-mail *enquiries@swiftwork.com*
contact Gill Hayward
www.swiftwork.com
Specialises in flexible working and work-life balance, helping organisations to capitalise on the challenges of new ways of working in the 21st century. Swiftwork provides a free membership forum for work returners, homeworkers and all people who are working, or want to work, flexibly. This includes online help and advice and a freelance directory for people who are available to work flexibly or part-time.

Totaljobs
e-mail *totaljobs.marketing@totaljobs.com*
www.totaljobs.com
One of the UK's busiest recruitment websites, *totaljobs.com* carries an average of 30,000 jobs across all major disciplines and industry

sectors. Jobseekers can post their CV on the site, apply for jobs online and have suitable jobs e-mailed direct to their inbox. Also offers useful advice to would-be women returners.

TrainingZone

e-mail *service@trainingzone.co.uk*
www.trainingzone.co.uk
Registration is free and provides access to an online network of 40,000 members. This site for training and HR professionals offers news, resources, and information on jobs. It also has listings of directories, professional services, and information on clients and markets.

Where Women Want to Work

Aurora Gender Capital Management
Albert Buildings
49 Queen Victoria Street
London EC4N 4SA
tel 020 7653 1909
fax 0709 228 7944
e-mail *info@auroravoice.com*
www.www2wk.com
One-stop shop for researching and comparing the companies that talented women want to work for. Information on how companies attract, develop and promote women and what makes a company good to work for.

J. LIBRARIES FOR WOMEN

Feminist Library Resource and Information Centre

5 Westminster Bridge Road
Southwark
London SE1 7XW
tel 020 7928 7789
Subscription library covering women and contemporary feminism in Britain and abroad. Holds books, pamphlets, journals and ephemera. Issues a quarterly newsletter. Open Tuesday, 11.00–20.00; Wednesday, 15.00–20.00; Saturday, 14.00–17.00.

Glasgow Women's Library
109 Trongate
Glasgow G1 5HD
tel/fax 0141 552 8345
e-mail *gwl@womens-library.org.uk*
www.womens-library.org.uk
Library of information for and about women. Consists of a reference
and lending library, an archive and resource centre. Also responsible
for Women at Work, the women's skills, services and business index,
their regularly updated database, a cuttings service and research
consultancy. Independent organisation with about 1,300 members.
Issues a newsletter and has a bulletin board; also runs free lifelong
learning courses and an adult literacy project.

The Women's Library
Old Castle Street
London E1 7NT
tel 020 7320 2222
fax 020 7320 2333
e-mail *enquirydesk@thewomenslibrary.ac.uk*
www.thewomenslibrary.ac.uk
A newly built centre consisting of a research library, exhibition hall
and education facilities and a café. The original library was
established in 1926 and run by the Fawcett Society until 1977 when
it moved to London Guildhall University. In 1988 a £4.2 million
Heritage Lottery grant enabled the university to build a new library. In
2002 London Guildhall University merged with the University of
North London to form London Metropolitan University. The Women's
Library contains 60,000 books and pamphlets dating from 1600 to the
present. There are three special printed collections and holdings
include periodical titles from 1745– , ephemera, more than 400
archive collections, and approximately 5,000 museum objects. Open
Tuesday, Wednesday and Friday, 9.30–17.00; Thursday, 9.30–
20.00; Saturday, 10.00–16.00.

K. WORK-LIFE BALANCE

Changing Direction
PO Box 164
Pinner
Middlesex HA5 3YL
tel 020 8868 7818
e-mail *dianawolfin@changingdirection.com*
www.changingdirection.com
Provides training, workshops and consultations for groups and individuals on all aspects of the return-to-work process, as well as coping strategies for work-life balance.

Department of Trade & Industry, Work-life balance campaign
e-mail *stephanie.ellis@dti.gsi.gov.uk*
www.2.dti.gov.uk/work-lifebalance
Aims to convince employers of the economic benefits of work-life balance and of the need for change. The campaign focuses on three main areas: tackling the long-hours culture; targeting sectors with acute work-life balance problems; providing support and guidance.

Flexecutive
Shropshire House
179 Tottenham Court Road
London W1T 7NZ
tel 020 7636 6744
e-mail *admin@flexecutive.co.uk*
www.flexecutive.co.uk
Founded in 1997 as the first recruitment agency offering flexible opportunities for senior staff. Aims to be the senior flexible answer to employers' recruitment problems and to employees' aspirations and wish for work-life balance. Has a 'working mum' factsheet on how to start working more flexibly; also has a job-share register.

New Ways to Work, *see* Working Families, page 231.

Parents at Work, *see* Working Familes, page 231.

Swiftwork
PO Box 120
Tunbridge Wells
TN5 7ZA
tel 01580 201 661
fax 01580 201 660
e-mail *enquiries@swiftwork.com*
contact Gill Hayward
www.swiftwork.com
Specialises in flexible working and work-life balance, helping organisations to capitalise on the challenges of new ways of working in the 21st century. Swiftwork provides a free membership forum for work returners, homeworkers and all people who are working, or want to work, flexibly. This includes online help and advice and a freelance directory for people who are available to work flexibly or part-time.

The Work Foundation
Peter Runge House
3 Carlton House Terrace
London SW1Y 5DG
tel 0870 165 6700
fax 0870 165 6701
e-mail *contactcentre@theworkfoundation.com*
www.theworkfoundation.com
Formerly the Industrial Society, an independent not-for-profit think-tank and consultancy with a large membership base. Conducts research, campaigning and practical interventions with the aim of improving productivity and quality of working life in the UK. Runs the Employers for Work-Life Balance website, which has practical advice, case studies and information on work-life issues for employers and policy-makers.

WLBC Ltd
The Work-Life Balance Standard
17 Packers Way
Misterton, Crewkerne
Somerset TA18 8NY

tel 01460 77713
e-mail *info@wlbc.ltd.uk*
www.wlbc.ltd.uk
A well-established consultancy working with all aspects of the work-life balance agenda, delivering services nationally. It offers custom-ised consultancy and a range of products and services including the Work-Life Balance Standard. It helps its clients to establish and implement an approach to work-life balance that works for them.

Working Families
1–3 Berry Street
London EC1V 0AA
tel 020 7253 7243
e-mail *office@workingfamilies.co.uk*
www.workingfamilies.org.uk
Formed in November 2003 when Parents at Work and New Ways to Work amalgamated under their new name. It is a campaigning charity that supports and gives a voice to working parents and carers, and helps employers create workplaces that encourage work-life balance. It holds best-practice seminars and training workshops around the country and runs the Employer of the Year Awards and the Best Boss competition. Free factsheets can be obtained by calling 020 7490 2414 and there is a freephone legal helpline on 0800 013 1313.

Work-Life Balance Trust
Gallery Zero One
Albert Road
Southsea
Hants PO5 2SF
tel 08707 577 266
fax 08707 577 272
e-mail *info@w-lb.org.uk*
www.w-lb.org.uk
Aims include: to challenge the long-hours cult, to update the workplace timetable and introduce flexible options, to ensure people-friendly policies work for business and to assist small businesses to implement work-life balance policies. Lobbies for good childcare for all and childcare tax breaks for working parents. Organises

conferences and seminars and carries out research. Promotes public awareness of work-life balance and advises government departments on the issues.

L. NETWORKING

Aurora Gender Capital Management
Albert Buildings
49 Queen Victoria Street
London EC4N 4SA
tel 020 7653 1909
fax 0709 228 7944
e-mail *admin@auroravoice.com*
www.network.auroravoice.com
Networking organisation for women-owned businesses. Aurora works to support women's individual business and career needs and also works at industry level to help companies throughout Europe to attract, retain, develop and advance women staff.

Black Women Mean Business (BWMB)
PO Box 11371
Stoke Newington
London N16 8TY
tel 020 7219 4426
e-mail *carbye@parliament.uk*
An initiative launched by Diane Abbott MP in 1993. She started the organisation as a way of helping black women business owners to develop the skills and expertise needed to become successful entrepreneurs. Initially BWMB consisted of professionals based within her constituency in Hackney, but now it has members from across London and from other parts of the UK. It is a non-profit-making organisation. Each year it hosts an annual reception for members as well as smaller workshops, seminars and specific one-off events, all with the aim of encouraging networking, sharing information and enhancing business acumen.

Capital Women's Forum
2 Greenways
Pembroke Road
Woking
Surrey GU22 7DY
tel 01483 720278
fax 01483 771932
e-mail *admin@CapitalWomen.co.uk*
www.CapitalWomen.co.uk
Offers women in the professions, senior management, sciences and the arts an opportunity to meet informally, exchange ideas and information and to network. It is now a national organisation with seven UK branches. Its mission statement reflects its objectives: to ensure that women's contribution and influence are recognised in the corridors of power, in the professions, industry or the arts and to achieve this by maintaining a forum in which successful women can develop professional and social contacts. Has partnership status on the Women's National Commission.

City Women's Network
Administrative Office
PO Box 353
Uxbridge UB10 0UN
tel 01895 272 178
e-mail *cwn@byword.org*
www.citywomen.org
Network for senior executive women in and around London. Members are professional women and business owners. Frequent meetings and workshops are held.

Focus Information Services
13 Prince of Wales Terrace
London W8 5PG
tel 020 7937 7799
helpline 020 7937 0050 (Monday to Thursday, 10.00–14.00)
fax 020 7937 9482
e-mail *office@focus-info.org*
www.focus-info.org

A non-profit organisation that supports international assignees and their families in the UK. Established in 1982, Focus provides information and networking opportunities for members, enabling them to integrate rapidly into their new environment. Among its services, Focus provides a career development programme to members. This programme offers comprehensive career assistance to accompanying partners in assignments in the UK, by teaching the basics of effective job searching and encouraging them to work in small groups.

Global Networker
e-mail *pat@global-networker.com*
www.global-networker.com
Offers two services to help spouses and partners of globally mobile employees to find work. Firstly, it runs networking events in London to help partners meet each other and potential employers, and to learn about networking and other job-search skills. Secondly, it runs a website with a range of useful reference information about job search in London, job search in other global capital cities, and general advice about portable careers. Global Networker can be contacted through its website.

Global Women Innovators and Inventors Network (GWIIN)
4 Waverley Gardens
Barking
Essex IG11 0BQ
tel 020 8591 9964
fax 020 8594 2811
e-mail *office@gwiin.com*
www.gwiin.com
Promotes the work of women in this field. It holds a conference, promotes education for children, makes awards and gives advice. GWIIN also holds exhibitions focusing on the importance of intellectual property rights and international trade.

Mumsnet
e-mail *contactus@mumsnet.com*
www.mumsnet.com
Set up by parents for parents to pool information, advice and
encouragement and discuss problems. Their first book, *Mums on
Babies*, a unique guide to the first year, based on the practical
experience of members, was published by Cassell Illustrated in 2003.
Mums on Pregnancy is due out in January 2004.

National Unit for Women's Enterprise
Scottish Enterprise
Small Business Services
150 Broomielaw
Atlantic Quay
Glasgow G2 8LU
tel 0141 248 2700
fax 0141 221 3217
e-mail *enquiries@scotent.co.uk*
www.scottishbusinesswomen.com
Targeted at women considering or in process of starting a business and
women running companies. This is a business support service offering
advice, mentors, skills training, etc. and the website is part of the
Women into Business Programme run by the Scottish Enterprise
Network and partners.

National Women's Register (NWR)
3a Vulcan House
Vulcan Road North
Norwich NR6 6AQ
tel 01603 406767; 0845 4500 287
fax 01603 407003
e-mail *office@nwr.org*
www.nwr.org
NWR is for making friends locally, exploring new interests and
meeting different women. It is a countrywide network of informal
groups that meet in each other's homes where lively-minded members
exchange ideas, enjoy challenging discussions and share social events
such as conferences and workshops.

Netmums
e-mail *enquiries@netmums.com*
www.netmums.com
Local information sites run by mums for mums to provide information and support for other local parents.

Older Feminists' Network
tel 020 8346 1900
email *beryl@bmdouglas.supanet.com*
www.ofn.org.uk
Formed 1982, meets regularly to give voice to the concerns of older women on ageism, sexism and their negative stereotypes. As well as monthly meetings, there are workshops and a newsletter.

Older Women's Network (OWN) – Europe
Via del Serraglio
10-06073 Corciano
PG, Italy
tel/fax (+39) 075 506 8006
e-mail *own@own-europe.org*
www.own-europe.org
Founded through the efforts of older women's groups participating in the three-year European Older Women's project initiated to celebrate the European Year of Older People in 1993. Aims to create opportunities for older women to participate in decision-making within their own communities or influence policy relating to issues such as pensions, health, housing and education.

UK-HRD
www.ukhrd.com
A free-to-join e-mail-based discussion forum for training, human resource and people development specialists. It comprises a moderated daily discussion digest e-mailed directly to those registered, where people ask questions, share experiences and discuss issues affecting them in their working lives. Around 8,000 people have registered to receive and contribute to the UK-HRD digests, ranging from experienced trainers to those working on their own. A membership site (paid) offers further

resources and benefits including the UK-HRD archive of all past discussion.

Women in Banking and Finance (WIBF)
43 Keswick Road
West Wickham
Kent BR4 9AS
tel 020 8777 6902
fax 020 8777 7064
e-mail *wibf_ann@btopenworld.com*
www.wibf.org.uk
Non-profit-making networking group founded in 1980 and sponsored by banks and city institutions. It aims to empower its members in the banking and finance industry to realise their full potential. WIBF provides a Personal Excellence Programme (incorporating personal development, mentoring and coaching, media and presentation skills and professional development), Networking Beyond Boundaries and a senior executive programme. An Awards for Achievement lunch, annual address and Speaker Series give access to leaders in the banking and finance industry. WIBF publishes a bimonthly newsletter and the above programmes are currently available in both London and Scotland.

Women In Business for Merseyside
e-mail *ellen.kerr@womeninbusiness.co.uk*
www.womeninbusiness.co.uk
Network that brings together and supports women in business, management, the professions and education and facilitates networking opportunities. Also provides business-relevant workshops. Launched in 1994 for women in the north-west.

Women in Docklands
Chair: Heather Waring
tel 020 8220 6919
e-mail *heather@waringwell.com*
Non-profit organisation set up in 1991 as a network for business women working or living in Docklands in East London. It welcomes business women from all areas of the capital and beyond, who wish

to expand their contacts in the region. Members range from sole traders to women in senior-level corporate posts, from the public, private and voluntary sectors.

Women's Environmental Network
PO Box 30626
London E1 1TZ
tel 020 7481 9004
fax 020 7481 9144
e-mail *info@wen.org.uk*
www.wen.org.uk
National membership charity educating, informing and empowering women and men who care about the environment. Network of local groups and campaigns on environment and health links, food and composting, real nappies, sanitary protection and waste prevention.

Women Returners' Network in association with the Grow Trust
Chelmsford College
Moulsham Street
Chelmsford CM2 0JQ
tel 01245 263796 (helpline)
e-mail *contact@women-returners.co.uk*
www.women-returners.co.uk
A national charity dealing with issues concerning women returners. Its aim is to provide innovative and practical support with a genuine 'hands-on' role to meeting the needs of clients. It provides a helpline for women who need advice and guidance.

M. MENTORING

Coaching and Mentoring Network
41–43 Oxford Road
Oxford OX4 4PF
tel 0870 733 3313
fax 0870 733 3314
e-mail *annabg@coachingnetwork.org.uk*
www.coachingnetwork.org.uk

Leading free and independent information and networking resource dedicated to coaching and mentoring. Provides help for both those interested in using and providing coaching and mentoring services. Includes articles, bookshop, news and events, online discussion forum and links to other useful services.

Institute of Business Advisers
Response House
Queen Street North
Chesterfield S41 9AB
tel 01246 453322
fax 01246 453300
e-mail *enquiries@iba.org.uk*
www.iba.org.uk
Non-profit professional institute for people specialising in helping small firms with business advice, counselling, mentoring and training. The institute is a registered charity and was founded in 1989.

Mentorset
e-mail *info@mentorset.org.uk*
www.mentorset.org.uk
Mentoring scheme for women in science, engineering or technology, sponsored by the Promoting SET for Women Unit of the DTI and industrial companies, organised by the Association of Women in Science and Engineering and the Women's Engineering Society. Hopes to increase the number of women who can maintain their SET careers and realise their potential.

National Mentoring Network
1st floor, Charles House
Albert Street
Eccles M30 0PW
tel 0161 787 8600
fax 0161 787 8100
e-mail *enquiries@nmn.org.uk*
www.nmn.org.uk
The network has 1,500 member organisations in the UK. Aims to promote the development of mentoring, offer advice and support to

those wishing to set up or develop mentoring programmes and provide a forum for the exchange of information and good practice. The network was set up in 1994 and is funded by membership fees and support from business and government departments. Members include colleges, career services, businesses, voluntary groups and others. It issues a network directory and other publications.

N. OVER FIFTIES

Age Positive
Age Positive Team
Department for Work and Pensions
Room W8d
Moorfoot
Sheffield S1 4PQ
e-mail *agepositive@dwp.gsi.gov.uk*
www.agepositive.gov.uk
The government campaign promoting age diversity in employment, increasing the retention of people over 50 in work and encouraging employers to use age-diverse practices. The website includes current news on age diversity, details of events, consultation, legislation and statistics on older workers. The campaign also publishes a code of practice.

Association of Retired and Persons Over Fifty (ARP/050)
Windsor House
1270 London Road
London SW16 4DH
tel 020 8764 3344
e-mail *info@arp050.org.uk*
www.arp050.org.uk
Social and campaigning association. Offers a range of member benefits, services, discounts and facilities for social gatherings. Has access to legislative bodies and decision-makers in UK and Europe.

Experience Corps
tel 0800 0157 441
www.experiencecorps.co.uk
An independent not-for-profit organisation operating throughout England, which has been set up with a grant-in-aid from the Home Office, specifically to encourage people over 50 to offer some of their time and experience actively to benefit their local communities.

FiftyOn
2nd floor, Ryder Court
Ryder Street
London SW1Y 6QB
tel 020 7451 0231
fax 020 7451 0456
e-mail *info@fiftyon.co.uk*
www.fiftyon.co.uk
Aims to be a voice for the over-50s on diversity, ageism and employment. Marketplace for jobs and career opportunities for job seekers over or nearly 50, and for employers valuing experience. Gives advice on finance, careers, health and leisure.

Maturity Works
Airport House
Purley Way
Croydon CR0 0XZ
tel 020 8667 0175
fax 020 8667 0558
email *enquiries@maturityworks.co.uk*
www.maturityworks.co.uk
Aims to promote better recruitment practice by employers and give the older worker access to the best opportunities available. As well as more than 300 advertised vacancies targeting work returners, the website also provides essential information and advice. It raises awareness of how age discrimination works and how to combat it. It also puts companies and older workers in touch with each other for their mutual benefit.

Older Feminists' Network
tel 020 8346 1900
email *beryl@bmdouglas.supanet.com*
www.ofn.org.uk
Formed 1982, meets regularly to give voice to the concerns of older women on ageism, sexism and their negative stereotypes. As well as monthly meetings, there are workshops and a newsletter.

Older Women's Network (OWN) – Europe
Via del Serraglio
10-06073 Corciano
PG, Italy
tel/fax (+39) 075 506 8006
e-mail *own@own-europe.org*
www.own-europe.org
Founded through the efforts of older women's groups participating in the three-year European Older Women's project initiated to celebrate the European Year of Older People in 1993. Aims to create opportunities for older women to participate in decision-making within their own communities or influence policy relating to issues such as pensions, health, housing and education.

Seniors Network
e-mail *mail305@seniorsnetwork.co.uk*
www.seniorsnetwork.co.uk
Network for adults (55+), their children, grandchildren and carers. Independent information resource for older people and their organisations. It covers computers, technology, finance, health, leisure, etc. and runs local seniors' forums and groups. Issues a newsletter.

Third Age Employment Network (TAEN)
207–221 Pentonville Road
London N1 9UZ
tel 020 7843 1590
fax 020 7843 1599
e-mail *taen@helptheaged.org.uk*
www.taen.org.uk

Has a membership of more than 200 organisations committed to helping mature people overcome barriers and realise their aims and ambitions. The membership represents many leading groups across the country delivering career change, advice, retraining and job-search support. TAEN plays a leading role in public policy on age, employment and retirement. See the website for a large amount of relevant information or contact TAEN for signposting to useful contacts.

Third Age Foundation
Britannia House
1 Glenthorne Road
London W6 0LH
tel 020 8748 9898
fax 020 8748 4250
e-mail *Sylvia@thirdage.org.uk*
www.thirdage.org.uk
Helps over-40s find a new direction, learn new skills and get back to work.

Common abbreviations

AAE – according to age and experience
AKA – also known as
AOB – any other business
AOL – America OnLine
APR – annual percentage rate
AWL – absent with leave
BTW – by the way
CAD – computer-aided design
CDL – career development loan
CEO – chief executive officer
CGI – computer-generated image
CGT – capital gains tax
COD – cash on delivery
COP – close of play
CPD – continuing professional development
CSA – Child Support Agency
CWO – cash with order
DfES – Department for Education and Skills
DTI – Department of Trade and Industry
ECDL – European Computer Driving Licence
ESF – European Social Fund
FAO – for the attention of
FAQ – frequently asked questions
FOTM – flavour of the month
FSA – Financial Services Authority
FTR – for the record
FWIW – for what it's worth

FYI – for your information
GBP – Great Britain pound (pound sterling)
GDP – gross domestic product (of a country)
HR – human resources (personnel)
IFA – independent financial adviser
IM(H)O – in my (humble) opinion
ISP – Internet service provider
JSA – Job Seeker's Allowance
N/A – not applicable
NI – National Insurance
NVQ – National Vocational Qualification
OLA – Outer London allowance
OLW – Outer London Weighting
OTE – on target earnings
PAYE – Pay As You Earn
PCM – per calendar month
PDQ – pretty damn quick
PIN – personal identification number
PLC – public limited company
POA – price on application
RSI – repetitive strain injury
RTF – rich text format (on computer documents)
SME – small and medium enterprises
SMP – Statutory Maternity Pay
SSP – Statutory Sick Pay
TBA – to be announced/arranged
TBC – to be confirmed
TLA – three letter acronym/abbreviation
TOS – temporarily out of stock
URL – uniform resource locator (used on websites)
USP – unique selling point
WLB – work-life balance
WPM – words per minute
WYSIWYG – what you see is what you get (computer screen images)

A suggested reading list

The following lists some books you may find useful. As well as the return to work, they also cover self-development.

Aslib Directory of Information Sources in the UK, 12th edition, 2002.

Back, Ken and Back, Kate, *Assertiveness at Work: A Practical Guide to Handling Awkward Situations*, 3rd edition, McGraw-Hill, 1999.

Birtles, Jasmine and Mack, Jane, *A Girl's Best Friend is Her Money: The 'Motley Fool' Woman's Investment Guide*, Boxtree, 2002.

Bolles, Richard N., *What Color is Your Parachute? A Practical Manual for Job-Hunters and Career-Changers*, revised edition, Ten Speed Press, 2003.

Bright, Jim and Earl, Joanne, *Brilliant CV: What Employers Want to See and How to Say It*, Prentice Hall, 2001.

Brittney, Lynn, *The Which? Guide to Working from Home: How to Make a Success of Your Home-Based Job or Business*, Which? Books, 2003.

Chapman, Andrew, *The Monster Guide to Jobhunting: Winning that Job with Internet Savvy*, Financial Times, Prentice Hall, 2001.

Corfield, Rebecca, *How You Can Get that Job: Application Forms and Letters Made Easy*, Kogan Page, 2003.

Corfield, Rebecca, *Preparing Your Own CV: How to Improve Your Chances of Getting the Job You Want*, new edition, Kogan Page, 2003.

Covey, Stephen R., Merrill, A. Roger and Merrill, Rebecca R., *First Things First: To Live, To Learn, To Leave a Legacy*, Simon & Schuster, 1994.

Covey, Stephen R., *The 7 Habits of Highly Effective People: Powerful Lessons in Personal Change*, Simon & Schuster, 1999.

Department for Education and Skills, Connexions, *Occupations 2004: The Essential Reference Book for Careers and Jobs*, Careers and Occupational Information Centre, 2004 (available looseleaf or on CD).

Dickson, Anne, *A Woman in Your Own Right*, reprinted by Quartet Books, 1992.

Directory of British Associations, CBD Research Ltd, sixteenth edition, 2002.

Dodds, Jill, *CVs and Interviews Made Easy*, Law Pack, 2002.

Essential Lifeskills series, includes: Davies, Philippa, *Thriving Under Pressure*; Quilliam, Susan, *Positive Thinking*; Thomas, David, *Improving Your Memory*, all Dorling Kindersley, 2003.

Essential Managers series, includes: Eaton, John and Johnson, Roy, *Coaching Successfully*, 2001; Heller, Robert and Hindle, Tim, *Reducing Stress*, 1998; Holden, Robert and Renshaw, Ben, *Balancing Work and Life*, 2002; Howard, Simon, *Creating a Successful CV*, 1999; all Dorling Kindersley.

Fisher, Roger and Ury, William, *Getting To Yes: Negotiating an Agreement Without Giving In*, 2nd edition, Random House, 1999.

Goleman, Daniel, *Emotional Intelligence: Why It Can Matter More Than IQ*, Bloomsbury, 1996.

Golzen, Godfrey and Reuvid, Jonathan, *A Guide to Working for Yourself*, 22nd edition, Kogan Page, 2003.

Golzen, Godfrey and Burrow, Colin, *Taking Up a Franchise*, 13th edition, Kogan Page, 2000.

Green, Graham, *The Career Change Handbook*, How To Books, 2003.

Hopson, Barrie and Scally, Mike, *Build Your Own Rainbow: A Workbook for Career and Life Management*, 3rd edition, Management Books 2000, 1999.

In a Week series, includes: Catt, Hilton and Scudamore, Pat, *Successful Job Applications In a Week*; Fleming, Peter, *Negotiating In a Week*; Mason, Roger, *Finance for Non-Financial Managers In a Week*, all Hodder & Stoughton, 2003.

Jackson, Tom and Jackson, Ellen, *The Perfect CV: How to Get the Job You Really Want*, Piatkus, 1996.

Jeffers, Susan, *Feel the Fear and Do It Anyway*, Arrow, 1991.

Jones, Alan, *How to Write a Winning CV: A Simple Step-By-Step Guide to Creating the Perfect CV*, 3rd edition, Random House, 2000.

Jones, Alan, *Winning at Interview: A New Way to Succeed*, Random House, 2000.

Lines, June, *30 Minutes . . . To Prepare a Job Application*, Kogan Page, 1997, reprinted 2003.

Pearson, Allison, *I Don't Know How She Does It: A Comedy About Failure, A Tragedy About Success*, Chatto and Windus, 2002, Vintage paperback 2003.

Pease, Allan, *Body Language*, Sheldon Press, 1992, new edition, Orion Books due December 2003.

Pease, Allan and Barbara, *Why Men Lie and Women Cry*, Orion Books, 2002.

Prior, Robert and Leibling, Mike, *Coaching Made Easy*, Kogan Page, 2003.

Roane, Susan, *How to Work a Room: The Ultimate Guide to Savvy Socialising and Networking*, Robson Books, 2002.

Segerman-Peck, Lily, *Networking and Mentoring: A Woman's Guide*, Piatkus, 1991 (out of print but available in public libraries). The author has booklets available on mentoring: *Essentials of Being a Better Mentor; Essentials of Setting Up a Mentoring Scheme; Essentials of Using Your Mentor Wisely*.

Semple, Andrea and Haig, Matt, *The Internet Job Search Handbook*, How To Books, 2001.

Taylor, Ros and Humphrey, John, *Fast Track to the Top: 10 Skills for Career Success*, Kogan Page, 2002.

Teach Yourself series, includes: Bird, Polly, *Time Management*; Shield, Daryl, *Flexible Working*; Turner, Mike, *Small Business Accounting*, all Hodder Arnold, 2003.

Timperley, John, *Negotiate Your Way to Success*, Piatkus, 2002.

The Which? Guide to Starting Your Own Business: How to Make a Success of Going It Alone, Which? Books, 2003.

Williams, Lynn, *30 Minutes . . . To Prepare The Perfect CV*, Kogan Page, 2002.

Woods, Ciara, *Everything You Need to Know at Work: A Complete Manual of Workplace Skills*, Prentice Hall, 2003.

Wright, Diana, *The Sunday Times Guide to Personal Finance*, HarperCollins, 2003.

Yate, Martin, *Great Answers to Tough Interview Questions*, 5th edition, Kogan Page, 2001.

Journals and magazines

Floodlight on Adult Learners' Week. Annual, May. Listing of events, open days, taster classes, talks, exhibitions and demonstrations. Available from colleges and libraries.

Opportunities: The Public Sector Recruitment and Career Development Weekly, Opportunities, Link House, West Street, Poole, Dorset BH15 1LL.

Primary Times. Free magazine for parents, pupils and staff of primary schools across the UK and Ireland; essentially a 'what's on' guide for families, supplemented with relevant editorials and advertising, and regular features on Returning to Work or Returning to Learning. It is a franchise, with each magazine owned by a local publisher/editor who invariably has a feel for the region he/she serves. Since it began, with one magazine in Bristol in 1989, the Primary Times group has grown to include over 40 regions of the UK and Ireland with over 1.6 million copies distributed via primary schools, sent home with the children to their parents or carers. For more information visit *www.primarytimes.net* or call 01491 411 416.

Index